Henry David Thoreau

THE RIVER

Selections from the *Journal* of Henry David Thoreau
Arranged with Notes by Dudley C. Lunt

Bramhall House • New York

The river is my own highway, the only wild
and unfenced part of the world hereabouts.

30 May 1852

COPYRIGHT © MCMLXIII BY TWAYNE PUBLISHERS, INC.
LIBRARY OF CONGRESS CATALOG CARD NUMBER: 62-19470
ALL RIGHTS RESERVED.
THIS EDITION IS PUBLISHED BY BRAMHALL HOUSE
A DIVISION OF CLARKSON N. POTTER, INC.
BY ARRANGEMENT WITH DUDLEY C. LUNT
A   B   C   D   E   F   G   H
MANUFACTURED IN THE UNITED STATES OF AMERICA

Contents

Introductory Note

It is when Thoreau is out on a river that he reaches the peak of his powers as a descriptive writer. This is amply attested by the popularity over nearly a century of his accounts of his river trips in the watersheds of the Penobscot and the Allagash that were assembled in *The Maine Woods* after his death. It is even more evident when the discursive digressions that interrupt *A Week on the Concord and Merrimack Rivers* are set to one side, and the reader may savour his relation of this riparian excursion as a piece of pastoral writing that is without a peer in the annals of American literature.

The Concord River sprawls across the countryside like a great Y lying on its side. Entering the township by its North and South Branches from the northwest and the southwest, it flows generally in a northeasterly direction leaving the town of Concord, in this view, on the right hand. The North Branch is the Assabet; the South, the Sudbury. Where the two conjoin at Nawshawtuct the stream becomes the Concord. This, in general, is the lay of the land.

Thus here close to hand was another element for the indulgence of the fierce insister upon his chosen way of life. A few feet of open water between him and the shore gave him a detachment that was valuable for its own sake. From a riparian point of view the world could be seen in new dimensions. The difference between afloat and ashore was vast. Out on the river in his boat Thoreau's powers of observation and his reflective mind merged in a fruitful union.

9

"I vastly increase my sphere and experience by a boat," he wrote.

The evidences of this lie scattered in the pages of his *Journal*. The purpose of this book is to bring some of them into the sequence of the seasons and thus to present in that framework a year of Thoreau's life on and along the Concord River. In the decade of regular entries in his *Journal* (1851-61) he usually put his boat in the water in the third week in March. This coincidence with the vernal equinox provides the point of departure. And hence this account starts with that event in the spring of the year and it continues on around until another spring, when again his boat is launched into that element from which he had been debarred during the winter months.

In this process the integrity of the text has been utterly respected, and for those who may wish to trace any passage to its source, a concordance has been supplied.

DUDLEY CAMMETT LUNT

The River

Spring

The ice of the night fills the river in the morning, and I hear it go grating downward at sunrise. As soon as I can get it painted and dried, I launch my boat and make my first voyage for the year up or down the stream, on that element from which I have been debarred for three months and a half. I taste a spring cranberry, save a floating rail, feel the element fluctuate beneath me, and am tossed bodily as I am in thought and sentiment. Then longen folk to gon on *voyages*.

The water freezes on the oars. I wish to hear my mast crack and see my rapt [?] boat run on her side, so low her deck drinks water and her keel plows air. My only competitors or fellow voyageurs are the musquash-hunters. To see a dead sucker washing on the meadows! The ice has broken up and navigation commenced. We may set sail for foreign

parts or expect the first arrival any day. To see the phenomena of the water and see the earth from the *water side,*
to stand outside of it on another element, and so to get a
pry on it in thought at least, that is no small advantage. I
make more boisterous and stormy voyages now than at any
season. . . . I vastly increase my sphere and experience
by a boat.

The river is now generally and rapidly breaking up. It
is surprising what progress has been made since yesterday.
It is now generally open about the town. It has gradually
worn and melted away at the bends, where it is shallow and
swift, and now small pieces are breaking off around the
edges and floating down these reaches. It is not generally
floated off, but dissolved and melted where it is, for the
open reaches gradually extend themselves till they meet,
and there is no space or escape for floating ice in any quantity, until the ice is all gone from the channel. I think that
what I have seen floating in former years is *commonly* such
as had risen up afterwards from the bottom of flooded
meadows. Sometimes, however, you observe great masses
of floating ice, consisting of that which is later to break up,
the thicker and more lasting ice from broad bays or between
bridges. There is now an open water passage on each side
of the broad field of ice in the bay above the railroad. The
water, which is rapidly rising, has overflowed the icy snow
on the meadows, which is seen a couple of feet beneath it,
for there is no true ice there. It is this rising of the water
that breaks up the ice more than anything.

*In the month of March, 1860, which was the last active
year of his life—Thoreau died in 1862—he inserted in his*
Journal *a relation of the general character of that month,
and his account of the 16th, which comprises the two opening paragraphs of this book, may be taken as typical of his
first day of the season on the river. In the years in which*

his regular day-to-day entries have survived—1852 through 1860—this usually occurred some time in the third week in March. But in the spring of 1856, following a long, cold winter of heavy snows, the ice barred him from the river until the 7th of April when he writes:

Launched my boat, through three rods of ice on the riverside, half of which froze last night. . . .

The first boat on the meadows is exciting as the first flower or swallow. It is seen stealing along in the sun under the meadow's edge. One breaks the ice before it with a paddle, while the other pushes or paddles, and it grates and wears against the bows.

We see Goodwin skinning the muskrats he killed this forenoon on bank at Lee's Hill, leaving their red and mutilated carcasses behind. He says he saw a few geese go over the Great Meadows on the 6th. The half of the meadows next the river, or more, is covered with snow ice at the bottom, which from time to time rises up and floats off. These and more solid cakes from over the river clog the stream where it is least broken up, bridging it quite over. Great cakes rest against every bridge. We were but just able to get under the stone arches by lying flat and pressing our boat down, after breaking up a large cake of ice which had lodged against the upper side.

Before we get to Clamshell, see Melvin ahead scare up two black ducks, which make a wide circuit to avoid both him and us. Sheldrakes pass also, with their heavy bodies. . . .

Melvin floats slowly and quietly along the willows, watching for rats resting there, his white hound sitting still and grave in the prow, and every little while we hear his gun announcing the death of a rat or two. The dog looks on understandingly and makes no motion.

To boat at Cardinal Shore and thence to Well Meadow and back to port. . . .

Hear the crack of Goodwin's piece close by, just as I reach my boat. He has killed another rat. Asks if I am bound upstream.

"Yes, to Well Meadow."

Says I can't get above the hay-path a quarter of a mile above on account of the ice; if he could, he'd 'a' been at Well Meadow before now. But I think I will try, and he thinks if I succeed he will try it. By standing on oars, which sink several inches, and hauling over one cake of ice, I manage to break my way into an open canal above, where I soon see three rats swimming. . . .

From opposite Bittern Cliff I pushed along with more or less difficulty to Well Meadow Brook. There was a water passage ten feet wide, where the river had risen beyond the edge of the ice, but not more than four or five feet was clear of the bushes and trees. . . . I shoved the ice on the one hand and the bushes and trees on the other all the way. Nor was the passage much wider below, as far back as where I had taken the boat. For all this distance the river *for the most part,* as well as all the pond was an unbroken field of ice. I went winding my way and scraping between the maples. Half a dozen rods off on the ice, you would not have supposed that there was room for a boat there. In some places you could have got on to the ice from the shore without much difficulty. But all of Well Meadow was free of ice. . . .

There in that slow, muddy brook near the head of Well Meadow, within a few rods of its source, where it winds amid the alders, which shelter the plants somewhat, while they are open enough now to admit the sun, I find two cowslips in full bloom, shedding pollen; and they may have opened two or three days ago; for I saw many conspicuous buds here on the 2nd which now I do not see. Have they been eaten off? Do we not often lose the earliest flowers thus? A little more, or if the river had risen as high as frequently, they would have been submerged.

What an arctic voyage was this in which I find the cowslips, the pond and river still frozen over for the most part as far down as Cardinal Shore! . . .

Noticed returning this afternoon, a muskrat sitting on the ice near a small hole in Willow Bay, so motionless and withal round and featureless, of so uniform a color, that half a dozen rods off I should not have detected him if not accustomed to observing them. Saw the same thing yesterday. It reminds me of the truth of the Indian's name for it—"that sits in a round form on the ice." You would think it was a particularly round clod of meadow rising above the ice. But while you look, it concludes its meditations or perchance its meal, and deliberately takes itself off through a hole at its feet and you see no more of it. . . .

The marsh hawks flew in their usual irregular low tacking, wheeling and circling flight, leisurely flapping and beating, now rising, now falling, in conformity with the contour of the ground. The last I think I have seen on the same beat in former years. He and his race must be well acquainted with the Musketicook and its meadows.[1] No

---

[1] The Indian name for the Concord River. Thoreau uses this and the word Musketaquid indiscriminately, and the explanation is to be found in *The Maine Woods.* In 1853, while "a-moose-hunting" along the West Branch of the Penobscot he was in camp at Northeast Carry one September evening with four Indians.

I asked our hosts what *Musketaquid,* the Indian name of Concord, Massachusetts, meant; but they changed it to *Musketicook,* and repeated that, and Tahmunt said that it meant Dead Stream, which is probably true. *Cook* appears to mean stream, and perhaps *quid* signifies the place or ground.

Four years later while traversing the length of Moosehead Lake in a birch, his Indian guide, Joe Polis, confirmed this:

I asked him the meaning of the word *Musketicook,* the Indian name of Concord River. He pronounced it *Muskeeticook,* emphasizing the second syllable with a peculiar guttural sound, and said that it meant "Dead-water," which it is, and in this definition he agreed exactly with the St. Francis Indian with whom I talked in 1853.

sooner is the snow off than he is back to his old haunts,
scouring that part of the meadows that is bare, while the
rest is melting. . . .

River had risen so since yesterday I could not get under
the bridge, but was obliged to find a round stick and roll
my boat over the road.

P.M.—Launch my boat and sail to Ball's Hill.

It is fine clear weather and a strong northwest wind. . . .
We sail over the Red [Hunt's] Bridge road. The water is
falling over the lower side of the road as over a dam. For
the road really operates as a dam, the water being much
lower on the east side.

A new phase of the spring is presented; a new season has
come. By the soaking rain and the wind of yesterday especially, the remaining snow and ice has been almost entirely swept away, and the ice has been broken, floated off,
and melted, and much frost taken out of the ground; and
now, as we glide over the Great Meadows before this
strong wind, we no longer see dripping, saturated russet
and brown banks through rain, hearing at intervals the alarm
notes of the early robins—banks which reflect a yellowish
light—but we see the bare and now pale brown and dry
russet hills. The earth has cast off her white coat and come
forth in her clean washed sober russet early spring dress.
As we look over the lively, tossing blue waves for a mile or
more eastward and northward, our eyes fall on these shining
russet hills, and Ball's Hill appears in this strong light at
the verge of this undulating blue plain, like some glorious
newly created island of the spring, just sprung up from the
bottom in the midst of the blue waters. The fawn-colored oak
leaves, with a few pines intermixed, thickly covering the
hill, look not like a withered vegetation, but an ethereal kind,
just expanded and peculiarly adapted to the season and
the sky.

Look toward the sun, the water is yellow, as water in which the earth has just washed itself clean of its winter impurities; look from the sun and it is a beautiful dark blue; but in each direction the crests of the waves are white, and you cannot sail or row over this watery wilderness without sharing the excitement of this element. Our sail draws so strongly that we cut through the great waves without feeling them. And all around, half a mile or a mile distant, looking over this blue foreground, I see the bare and peculiarly neat, clean-washed, and bright russet hills reflecting the bright light (after the storm of yesterday) from an infinite number of dry blades of withered grass. The russet surfaces have now, as it were, a combed look—combed by the rain. . . .[2]

We meet one great gull beating up the course of the river against the wind, at Flint's Bridge—one says they were seen about a week ago, but there was very little water then. Its is a very leisurely sort of limping flight, tacking its way along like a sailing vessel, yet the slow security with which it advances suggests a leisurely contemplativeness in the birl, as if it were working out some problem quite at its leisure. As often as its very narrow, long, and curved wings are lifted up against the light, I see a very narrow distinct light edging to the wing where it is thin. . . . Afterwards, from Ball's Hill, looking north, I see two more circling about looking for food over the ice and water.

By the river, see distinctly red-wings and hear their *conqueree*. They are not associated with grackles. They are an age before their cousins, have attained to clearness and liquidity. They are officers, epauletted; the others are rank and file. I distinguish one even by its flight, hovering slowly

---

[2] The period between the time when the snow commenced to disappear and before the frost was out of the ground, Thoreau referred to as "the peculiar and interesting *Brown Season* of the spring."

from tree-top to tree-top, as if ready to utter its liquid notes. Their whistle is very clear and sharp, while the grackle's is ragged and split.

Morning along the river.

The air full of song sparrows—*swedit swedit swedit* and then a rapid jingle or trill, holding up its head without fear of me, the innocent, humble bird, or one pursuing another through the alders by the waterside. Why are the early birds found most along the water? These song sparrows are now first heard *commonly*. The blackbirds, too, create some melody. And the bluebirds, how sweet their warble in the soft air, heard over the water! The robin is heard further off, and seen flying rapidly, hurriedly through the orchard.

I go along the riverside to see the now novel reflections. The subsiding waters have left a thousand little isles, where willows and sweet-gale and the meadow itself appears. I hear the phoebe note of the chickadee, one taking it up behind another as in a catch, *phee-bee phe-bee*. The very earliest alder is in bloom and sheds its pollen. I detect a few catkins at a distance by their distinct yellowish color. This is the first native flower.

Overcast and cold. Yet there is quite a concert of birds along the river; the song sparrows are very lively and musical, and the blackbirds already sing *o-gurgle-ee-e-e* from time to time on the top of a willow or elm or maple, but oftener a sharp, shrill whistle or *tchuck*. I also hear a short, regular robin song, though many are flitting about with hurried note. The bluebird faintly warbles, with such ventriloquism that I thought him further off. He requires a warmer air. The jays scream. I hear the downy woodpecker's rapid tapping and *my* first distinct spring note (*phe-be*) of the chickadee.

P.M.—Paddle to the Bedford line.

It is now high time to look for arrowheads, etc. I spend many hours every spring gathering the crop which the melting snow and rain have washed bare. When, at length, some island in the meadow or some sandy field elsewhere has been plowed, perhaps for rye, in the fall, I take note of it, and do not fail to repair thither as soon as the earth begins to be dry in the spring. If the spot chances never to have been cultivated before, I am the first to gather a crop from it. The farmer little thinks that another reaps a harvest which is the fruit of his toil. As much ground is turned up in a day by the plow as Indian implements could not have turned over in a month, and my eyes rest on the evidences of an aboriginal life which passed here a thousand years ago perchance. Especially if the knolls in the meadows are washed by a freshet where they have been plowed the previous fall, the soil will be taken away lower down and the stones left—the arrowheads, etc., and soapstone pottery amid them—somewhat as gold is washed in a dish or tom.[3] . . . As much as sportsmen go in pursuit of ducks, and gunners of musquash, and scholars of rare books, and travelers of adventures, and poets of ideas, and all men of money, I go in search of arrowheads when the proper season comes round again. . . .

As we were paddling over the Great Meadows, I saw at a distance, high in the air above the middle of the meadow, a very compact flock of blackbirds advancing against the sun. Though there were more than a hundred, they did not appear to occupy more than six feet in breadth, but the whole flock was dashing first to the right and then to the left. When advancing straight toward me and the sun, they made but little impression on the eye—so many fine dark points merely, seen against the sky—but as often as they

---

[3] A tom was a trough in which miners washed their pay dirt. Thoreau knew the cant of the forty-niner.

wheeled to the right or left, displaying their wings flatwise and the whole length of their bodies, they were a very conspicuous black mass.

This fluctuation in the amount of dark surface was a very pleasing phenomenon. It reminded me [of] those blinds whose sashes (*sic*) are made to move all together by a stick, now admitting nearly all the light and now entirely excluding it; so the flight of blackbirds opened and shut. But at length they suddenly spread out and dispersed, some flying off this way, and others that, as when a wave strikes against a cliff, it is dashed upward and lost in a fine spray. So they lost their compactness and impetus and broke up suddenly in mid-air.

We see eight geese floating afar in the middle of the meadow, at least half a mile off, plainly (with glass) much larger than the ducks in their neighborhood and the white on their heads very distinct. When at length they arise and fly off northward, their peculiar *heavy* undulating wings, blue-heron-like and unlike any duck, are very noticeable. The black, sheldrake, etc., move their wings rapidly, and remind you of paddle-wheel steamers. Methinks the wings of the black duck appear to be set very far back when it is flying. The meadows, which are still covered far and wide, are quite alive with black ducks.

When walking about on the low east shore at the Bedford bound, I heard a faint honk, and looked around over the water with my glass, thinking it came from that side or perhaps from a farmyard in that direction. I soon heard it again, and at last we detected a great flock passing over, quite on the other side of us and pretty high up. From time to time one of the company uttered a short note, that peculiarly metallic, clangorous sound. These were in a single undulating line, and, as usual, one or two were from time to time crowded out of the line, apparently by the crowding of those in the rear, and were flying on one side and trying to recover their places, but at last a second short line was formed, meeting the long one at the usual angle and making a figure somewhat like a hay-hook. . . .

The great gulls fly generally up or down the river valley, cutting off the bends of the river, and so do these geese. These fly sympathizing with the river—a stream in the air, soon lost in the distant sky. . . .

Ball's Hill, with its withered oak leaves and its pines, looks very fair today, a mile and a half across the water, through a very thin varnish or haze. It reminds me of the isle which was called up from the bottom of the sea, which was given to Apollo. . . . Today we sail swiftly on dark rolling waves or paddle over a sea as smooth as a river, unable to touch the bottom, where mowers work and hide their jugs in August; coasting the edge of maple swamps, where alder tassels and white maple flowers are kissing the tide that has risen to meet them. But this particular phase of beauty is fleeting. Nature has so many shows for us she cannot afford to give much time to this. In a few days, perchance, these lakes will have all run away to the sea. . . .

Here, where in August the bittern booms in the grass, and mowers march *en echelon* and whet their scythes and crunch the ripe wool-grass, raised now a few feet, you scud before the wind in your tight bark and listen to the surge (or sough?) of the great waves sporting around you, while you hold the steering-oar and your mast bends to the gale and you stow all your ballast to windward. The crisped sound of surging waves that rock you, that ceaseless roll and gambol, and ever and anon break into your boat.

Deep lie the seeds of the rhexia now, absorbing wet from the flood, but in a few months this mile-wide lake will have gone to the other side of the globe; and the tender rhexia will lift its head on the drifted hummocks in dense patches, bright and scarlet as a flame—such succession have we here —where the wild goose and countless wild ducks have floated and dived above them. So Nature condenses her matter. She is a thousand thick. So many crops the same surface bears.

Undoubtedly the geese fly more numerously over rivers which, like ours, flow northeasterly—are more at home with the water under them. Each flock runs the gauntlet of a thousand gunners, and when you see them steer off from you and your boat you may remember how great their experience in such matters may be, how many such boats and gunners they have seen and avoided between here and Mexico, and even now, perchance (though you, low plodding, little dream it), they see one or two more lying in wait ahead. They have an experienced ranger of the air for their guide. The echo of one gun hardly dies away before they see another pointed at them. . . .[4]

I see with my glass as I go over the railroad bridge, sweeping the river, a great gull standing far away on the top of a muskrat cabin which rises just above the water opposite the Hubbard Bath. When I get round within sixty rods of him, ten minutes later, he still stands on the same spot, constantly turning his head to every side, looking out for foes. Like a wooden image of a bird he stands there, heavy to look at; head, breast, beneath, and rump pure white; slate-colored wings tipped with black and extending beyond the tail—the herring gull. I can see clear down to its webbed feet. But now I advance, and he rises easily, goes off northeastward over the river with a leisurely flight.

---

[4] This refers to the former custom of spring shooting. A century ago, there were few game laws, and migrating wild fowl were shot in both the fall and the spring of the year. The first partial curtailment of spring shooting in Massachusetts came in 1870, but the situation was not brought under full control until 1909 when, largely through the efforts of Edward Howe Forbush, the author of the celebrated *Birds of Massachusetts,* an act was passed prohibiting it altogether.

A pleasant short voyage is that to the Leaning Hemlocks on the Assabet, just round the Island under Nawshawtuct Hill. The river here has in the course of ages gullied into the hill, at a curve, making a high and steep bank, on which a few hemlocks grow and overhang the deep eddying basin. For as long as I can remember, one or more of these has always been slanting over the stream at various angles, being undermined by it, until one after another, from year to year, they fall in and are swept away. This is a favorite voyage for ladies to make, down one stream and up the other, plucking the lilies by the way and landing on the Island, and concluding with a walk on Nawshawtuct Hill.

A long March voyage upstream was that to the Sudbury Meadows and through them beyond the western bound of Concord. This is described in the opening pages of A Week on the Concord and Merrimack Rivers, *Thoreau's first book, published in 1849, which he interleaved with his early essays, poems and philosophical dissertations. The following excerpts have been taken from the modern abridged edition published in Boston in 1954 under the title* The Concord and the Merrimack.

In Concord, it [the river] is in summer from four to fifteen feet deep, and from one hundred to three hundred feet wide, but in the spring freshets, when it overflows its banks, it is in some places nearly a mile wide. Between Sudbury and Wayland the meadows acquire their greatest breadth, and when covered with water, they form a handsome chain of shallow vernal lakes, resorted to by numerous gulls and ducks. Just above Sherman's Bridge between these towns, is the largest expanse; and when the wind blows freshly in a raw March day, heaving up the surface into dark and sober billows or regular swells, skirted as it is in the distance with alder-swamps and smoke-like maples, it looks like a smaller Lake Huron, and is very pleasant and exciting for a landsman to row or sail over.

The farm-houses along the Sudbury shore, which rises gently to a considerable height, command fine water prospects at this season. The shore is more flat on the Wayland side, and this town is the greatest loser by the flood. . . .

It is worth the while to make a voyage up this stream, if you go no farther than Sudbury, only to see how much country there is in the rear of us; great hills, and a hundred brooks, and farm houses, and barns, and haystacks you never saw before, and men everywhere; Sudbury that is *Southborough* men, and Wayland, and Nine-Acre-Corner men, and Bound Rock, where four towns bound on a rock in the river, Lincoln, Wayland, Sudbury, and Concord.

Many waves are there agitated by the wind, keeping nature fresh, the spray blowing in your face, reeds and rushes waving; ducks by the hundred, all uneasy in the surf, in the raw wind, just ready to rise, and now going off with a clatter and a whistling like riggers straight for Labrador, flying against the stiff gale with reefed wings, or else circling round first, with all their paddles briskly moving, just over the surf, to reconnoitre you before they leave these parts; gulls wheeling overhead, muskrats swimming for dear life, wet and cold, with no fire to warm them by that you know of, their labored homes rising here and there like haystacks; and countless mice and moles and winged titmice along the sunny, windy shore; cranberries tossed on the waves and heaving up on the beach, their little red skiffs beating about among the alders—such healthy natural tumult as proves the last day is not yet at hand. And there stand all around the alders, and birches, and oaks, and maples full of glee and sap, holding in their buds until the waters subside.

You shall perhaps run aground on Cranberry Island, only

some spires of last year's pipe-grass above water to show where the danger is, and get as good a freezing there as anywhere on the Northwest Coast. I never voyaged so far in all my life. You shall see men you never heard of before, whose names you don't know, going away down through the meadows with long ducking-guns, with water-tight boots wading through the fowl-meadow grass, on bleak, wintry, distant shores, with guns at half-cock; and they shall see teal—blue-winged, green-winged—sheldrakes, whistlers, black ducks, ospreys, and many other wild and noble sights before night, such as they who sit in parlors never dream of.

I hear late tonight the unspeakable rain, mingled with rattling snow against the windows, preparing the ground for spring.

April

A warm, dripping rain, heard on one's umbrella as on a snug roof, and on the leaves without, suggests comfort. We go abroad with a slow but sure contentment, like turtles under their shells. We never feel so comfortable as when we are abroad in a storm with satisfaction. Our comfort is positive then. We are all compact, and our thoughts collected. We walk under the clouds and mists as under a roof. Now we seem to hear the ground a-soaking up the rain. . . . How the thirsty grass rejoices! It has pushed up so visibly since morning, and fields that were completely russet yesterday are already tinged with green. We rejoice with the grass.

I hear the hollow sound of drops falling into the water under Hubbard's Bridge, and each one makes a conspicuous bubble which is floated downstream. Instead of ripples there are a myriad dimples on the stream.

Starlight by river up Assabet. . . .

Without a mist the river appears indefinitely wide. Looking westward the water, still reflecting the twilight, appears
elevated, and the shore-line, being invisible, lost against the
distant highland, is referred toward the highland against
which it is seen, for the slope of the hill and the expanse of
the meadow cannot be appreciated, appearing only edgewise as height. We therefore make the water, which extends
but a rod or two, wash the base of hills a quarter of a mile
distant. There are but three elements in the landscape now
—the star-studded sky, the water, reflecting the stars and
the lingering daylight, and the dark but comparatively
narrow land between. At first there was no fog.

Hear ducks, disturbed, make a quacking or loud croaking. Now, at night, the scent of muskrats is very strong in
particular localities. Next to the skunk, it is perceived further than that of any of our animals that I can think of.
I perceive no difference between this and the musk with
which ladies scent themselves, though here I pronounce it
a strong, rank odor. In the faint reflected twilight, I distinguish one rapidly swimming away from me, leaving a
widening ripple behind, and now hear one plunge from
some willow or rock. A faint croaking from over the meadow
up the Assabet, exactly like frogs. . . . Now and then, when
I pass an opening in the trees which line the shore, I am
startled by the reflection of some bright star from a bay.

6 A.M.—To the riverside and Merrick's Pasture.

The sun is up. The water on the meadows is perfectly
smooth and placid, reflecting the hills and clouds and trees.
The air is full of the notes of birds—song sparrows, redwings,
robins (singing a strain), bluebirds—and I hear also a lark
—as if all the earth had burst forth into song. The influence
of this April morning has reached them, for they live out-
of-doors all the night, and there is no danger that they will

oversleep themselves such a morning. . . . As a fair day is promised, and the waters are falling decide to go to the Sudbury meadows with C.,[1] 9 A.M. . . .

The Charles Miles Run full and rumbling. The water is the color of ale, here dark red ale over the yellow sand, there yellowish frothy ale where it tumbles down. Its foam, composed of large white bubbles, makes a kind of arch over the rill, snow white and contrasting with the general color of the stream while the latter ever runs under it carrying the lower bubbles with it and new ones ever supply their places. At least eighteen inches high, this stationary arch. I do not remember elsewhere such highly colored water. It drains a swamp nearby and is dry the greater part of the year. Coarse bubbles continually bursting. A striped snake by the spring and a black one. The grass here is delightfully green while there is no fresh green anywhere else to be seen. It is the most refreshing of all colors. It is what all the meadows will soon be. The color of no flower is so grateful to the eye. . . .

After coming in sight of Sherman's Bridge, we moored our boat by sitting on a maple twig on the east side to take a leisurely view of the meadow. The eastern shore here is a fair specimen of New England fields and hills, sandy and barren but agreeable to my eye, covered with withered grass on their rounded slopes and crowned with low reddish bushes, shrub oaks. There is a picturesque group of eight oaks near the shore, and through a thin fringe of wood I see some boys driving home an ox-cartload of hay. . . .

In upsetting the boat, which has been newly tarred, I have got some tar on my hands, which imparts to them on

---

[1] William Ellery Channing was Thoreau's most frequent companion. He accompanied him on his excursions to Cape Cod in October, 1849, and July, 1855, and with Sophia Thoreau he edited the first edition of *The Maine Woods* (1864) and of *Cape Cod* (1865). He was the author of *Thoreau —The Poet-Naturalist*.

the whole an agreeable fragrance. This exercise of the arms and chest after a long winter's stagnation, during which only the legs have labored, . . . is perhaps the greatest value of these paddling excursions. I see, far in the south, the upright black piers of the bridge just rising above the water. They are more conspicuous than the sleepers and the rails. The occasional patches of snow on the hillsides are unusually bright by contrast; they are landmarks to steer by. . . .

Landed on Tull's Island. . . . The staddles,[2] from which the hay has been removed, rise a foot or two above the water. Large white gulls are circling over the water. The shore of this meadow lake is quite wild, and in most places low and rather inaccessible to walkers. On the rocky point of this island, where the wind is felt, the waves are breaking merrily, and now for half an hour our dog has been standing in the water under the small swamp white oaks, and ceaselessly snapping at each wave as it broke, as if it were a living creature. He, regardless of cold and wet, thrusts his head into each wave to gripe it. . . . He then rolls himself in the leaves for a napkin. We hardly set out to return when the water looked sober and rainy. There was more appearance of rain in the water than in the sky—April weather look. And soon we saw the dimples of drops on the surface. I forgot to mention before the cranberries seen on the bottom, as we pushed over the meadows, and the red beds of pitcher-plants. . . .

Return to our boat. We have to go ashore and upset it every half-hour, it leaks so fast, for the leak increases as it sinks in the water in geometrical progression. I see, among the phenomena of spring, here and there a dead sucker floating on the surface, perhaps dropped by a fish hawk or a gull, for the gulls are circling this way overhead to re-

---

[2] Staddles are the time-blackened stakes that still stand out to catch the eye in its sweeping of many a New England marsh, but the conical cocks of marsh hay they once supported belong to an earlier day.

connoitre us. They will come sailing overhead to observe us.
On making the eastward curve in the river, we find a strong
wind against us. Pushing slowly across the meadow in front
of the Pantry, the waves beat against the bows and sprinkle
the water half the length of the boat. The froth is in long
white streaks before the wind, as usual striping the surface. . . .

The rain now turns to snow with large flakes, so soft
many cohere in the air as they fall. They make us white as
millers and wet us through, yet it is clear gain. I hear a
solitary hyla for the first time. At Hubbard's Bridge count
eight ducks going over. Had seen one with outstretched
neck over the Great Meadows in Sudbury. Looking up, the
flakes are black against the sky. And now the ground begins to whiten. Get home at 5:30 P.M.

About 9 A.M., C. and I paddle down the river. . . .

Approaching the island we hear the air full of the hum
of bees, which at first we refer to the near trees. It comes
from the white maples across the North Branch [Assabet],
fifteen rods off. We hear it from time to time as we paddle
along all day down to the Bedford line. There is no pause
to the hum of the bees all this warm day. It is a very simple
but pleasing and soothing sound, this susurrus, this early in
the spring. When off the mouth of the Mill Brook we hear
the stertorous *tut tut tut* of frogs from the meadow with an
occasional faint bullfrog-like *er er er* intermingled. . . .

There, too, are countless painted turtles out, around on
the banks and hummocks left by the ice. Their black and
muddy backs shine afar in the sun, and though now fifteen
to twenty rods off, I see through my glass that they are
already alarmed, have their necks stretched out and are
beginning to slip into the water, where many heads are seen.
Resolved to identify this frog, one or two of whose heads

I could already see above the surface with my glass, I picked my way to the nearest pool. Close where I landed an *R. halecina* lay out on some sedge. In went all the turtles immediately, and soon after the frogs sank to the bottom, and their note was heard only from more distant pools. I stood perfectly still, and ere long they began to reappear one by one, and spread themselves out on the surface. . . .

Gradually they begin to recover their voices but it is hard to say at first which one of the dozen within twenty feet is speaking. They begin to swim and hop along the surface toward each other. Their note is a hard dry *tut tut tut tut,* not at all ringing like the toad's, and produced with very little *swelling* or motion of the throat, but as much trembling of the whole body; and from time to time one makes a faint somewhat bullfrog-like *er er er.* Both these sounds, then, are made by one frog, and what I have formerly thought an early bullfrog note was this. . . .

This sound we continue to hear all day long, especially from the broad meadows in Bedford. Close at hand a single one does not sound loud, yet it is surprising how far a hundred or thousand croaking (?) at once can be heard. It comes borne on the breeze from north over the Bedford meadows a quarter of a mile off, filling the air. It is like the rattling of a wagon along some highway, or more like a distant train on a railroad, or else of many rills emptying in, or more yet like the sound of a factory, and it comes with an echo which makes it seem yet more distant and universal. At this distance it is a soft and almost purring sound, yet with the above-named bullfrog-like variation in it.

Sometimes the meadow will be almost still; then they will begin in earnest, and plainly excite one another into a general snoring or eructation over a quarter of mile of meadow. It is unusually early [April 3, 1858] to hear them so numerously, and by day, but the water being so very low

and shallow on the meadows, is unusually warm this pleasant day. This might be called the Day of the Snoring Frogs,
or the Awakening of the Meadows.

Frogs are strange creatures. One would describe them as
peculiarly wary and timid, another as equally bold and
imperturbable. All that is required in studying them is patience. You will sometimes walk a long way along a ditch
and hear twenty or more leap in one after another before
you, and see where they rippled the water, without getting
sight of one of them. Sometimes, as this afternoon the two
R. fontinalis, when you approach a pool or spring a frog
hops in and buries itself at the bottom. You sit down on
the brink and wait patiently for his reappearance. After a
quarter of an hour or more he is sure to rise to the surface
and put out his nose quietly without making a ripple, eyeing
you steadily. At length he becomes as curious about you
as you can be about him. He suddenly hops straight toward
[you], pausing within a foot, and takes a near and leisurely
view of you. Perchance you may now scratch its nose with
your finger and examine it to your heart's content, for it is
become as impurturbable as it was shy before. You conquer
them by superior patience and immovableness; not by
quickness, but by slowness; not by heat, but by coldness.
You see only a pair of heels disappearing in the weedy
bottom, and, saving a few insects, the pool becomes as
smooth as a mirror and apparently as uninhabited. At length,
after half an hour, you detect a frog's snout and a pair of
eyes above the green slime, turned toward you. . . .

As I go down the street just after sunset, I hear many
snipe tonight. This sound is annually heard by the villagers,
but always at this hour, *i.e.* in the twilight—a hovering
sound high in the air—and they do not know what to refer
it to. It is very easily imitated by the breath. A sort of shud-

dering with the breath. It reminds me of calmer nights. Hardly one in a hundred hears it, and perhaps not nearly so many know what creature makes it. Perhaps no one dreamed of snipe an hour ago but the air seemed empty of such as they; but as soon as the dusk begins, so that a bird's flight is concealed, you hear this peculiar spirit-suggesting sound, now far, now near, heard through and above the evening din of the village.

I landed on Merrick's pasture near the rock, and when I stepped out of the boat and drew it up, a snipe flew up and lit again seven or eight rods off. After trying in vain for several minutes to see it on the ground there, I advanced a step, and to my surprise, scared up two more which had squatted on the bare meadow all the while within a rod, while I drew up my boat and made a good deal of noise. In short I scared up twelve, one or two at a time, within a few rods which were feeding on the edge of the meadow just laid bare, each rising with a sound like *squeak squeak*, hoarsely. That part of the meadow seemed all alive with them. It is almost impossible to see one on the meadow, they squat and run so low and are so completely the color of the ground.

I see half a dozen sheldrakes very busily fishing around the base of Lupine Hill or Promontory. There are two full-plumaged males and the rest females, or perhaps some of them young males. They are coasting along swiftly with their bodies sunk low and their heads half under, looking for their prey, one behind another, frequently turning and passing over the same ground again. Their crests are very conspicuous, thus: [sketch] When one sees a fish he at first swings rapidly after it, and then, if necessary, flies close over the water after it, and this excites all the rest to follow, swimming or flying, and if one seizes the fish, which I suspect is commonly a pickerel, they all pursue the lucky fisher, and he makes the water fly far in his efforts to get away and gulp down his fish. I can see the fish in his bill all the while, and he must swallow it very skilfully and quickly, if at all.

I was first attracted to them by seeing these great birds rushing, shooting, thus swiftly through the air and water and throwing the water high about them. Sometimes they dive and swim quietly beneath, looking for their game. At length they spy me or my boat, and [I] hear a faint quack indicative of alarm, and suddenly all arise and go off.

I am delighted to find a perfect specimen of the *Mergus merganser*, or goosander, undoubtedly shot yesterday by the Fast-Day sportsmen. . . . It is a perfectly fresh and very beautiful bird, and as I raise it, I get sight of its long, slender vermilion bill—color of red sealing wax—and its clean bright orange legs and feet, and then of its perfectly smooth and spotlessly pure white breast and belly, tinged with a faint salmon, or tinged with a delicate buff inclining to salmon. . . .

I skinned my duck yesterday. . . . It is wonderful that a man, having undertaken such an enterprise, ever persevered in it to the end, and equally wonderful that he succeeded. To skin a bird, drawing backward, wrong side out, over the legs and wings down to the base of the mandibles! Who would expect to see a smooth feather again? This skin was very tender on the breast. I should have done better had I stuffed it at once or turned it back before the skin became stiff. Look out not to cut the ear and eyelid.

But what a pot-bellied thing is a stuffed bird compared even with the fresh dead one I found! It looks no longer like an otter, like a swift diver, but a mere waddling duck.

Going through Dennis's field with C. saw a flock of geese on east side of river near willows. Twelve great birds on the troubled surface of the meadows, delayed by the storm.

We lay on the ground behind an oak and our umbrella, eighty rods off, and watched them. Soon we heard a gun go off, but could see no smoke in the mist and rain. And the whole flock rose, spreading their great wings and flew with clangor[3] a few rods and lit in the water again, then swam swiftly toward our shore with outstretched necks. I knew them first from ducks by their long necks. Soon appeared the man, running toward the shore in vain. . . .

We remained close under our umbrella by the tree, ever and anon looking through a peep-hole between the umbrella and the tree at the birds. On they came, sometimes in two, sometimes in three, squads, warily, till we could see the steel-blue and green reflections from their necks. We held the dog close the while—C. lying on his back in the rain, had him in his arms—and thus we gradually edged round on the ground in this cold, wet, windy storm, keeping our feet to the tree, and the great wet calf of a dog with his eyes shut so meekly in our arms. We laughed well at our adventure. Occasionally one expanded a gray wing. They swam fast and warily, seeing our umbrella. They showed white on breasts. And not till after half an hour, sitting cramped and cold and wet on the ground, did we leave them.

Trying the other day to imitate the honking of geese, I found myself flapping my sides with my elbows, as with wings, and uttering something like the syllables *mow-ack* with a nasal twang and twist in my head, and I produced their note so perfectly in the opinion of the hearers that I thought I might possibly draw a flock down.[4]

---

[3] The "honk" of the goose [Thoreau].

[4] Only those who can control the breaking of their voices can call geese. It is a peculiar kind of yodel—a gutteral *aah*. Next the break, and then the nasal *ooh*. Those skilled in the art— and it is an art, for the correct timing demands a knowledge of their habits born of long observation—can call them down out of the sky until they come in to hover over the decoys, and set their great wings to pitch. No sport is the equal of this in the intensity of its thrilling suspense.

P.M.—Up Assabet with [Minot] Pratt.

Standing under the north side of the hill, I hear the rather innocent *phe phe, phe phe, phe phe, phe'* of a fish hawk (for it is not a scream, but a rather soft and innocent note), and, looking up, see one come sailing from over the hill. The body looks quite short in proportion to the spread of the wings, which are quite dark or blackish brown. He evidently has something in his talons. We soon after disturb him again, and, at length after circling around over the hill and adjacent fields, he alights in plain sight on one of the half-dead white oaks on the top of the hill where probably he sat before.

As I look through my glass, he is perched on a large dead limb and is evidently standing on a fish (I had noticed something in his talons as he flew), for he stands high and uneasily, finding it hard to keep his balance in the wind. He is disturbed by our neighborhood and does not proceed at once to eat his meal. I see the tail of the fish hanging over the end of the limb. Now and then he pecks at it. I see the white on the crown of the hawk. It is a very large black bird as seen against the sky. Soon he sails away again, carrying his fish as before, horizontally beneath his body, and he circles about over the adjacent pasture like a hawk hunting, though he can only be looking for a suitable place to eat his fish or waiting for us to be gone.

Looking under the limb on which he was perched, we find a piece of the skin of a sucker (?) or some other scaly fish which a hawk had dropped there long since. No doubt many a fish hawk has taken his meal on that sightly perch. It seems then, that the fish hawk which you see soaring and sailing so leisurely over the land—for this one soared quite high into the sky at one time—may have a fish in his talons all the while and only be waiting till you are gone for an opportunity to eat it on his accustomed perch.

April 20. Rain, rain, rain—a northeast storm. I see that it is raising the river somewhat again. Some little islets which had appeared on the meadow northwest of Dodd's are now fast being submerged again.

April 22. It has rained two days and nights, and now the sun breaks out, but the wind is still easterly, and the storm probably is not over. In a few minutes the air is full of mizzling rain again.

8 A.M.—Go to my boat opposite Bittern Cliff. . . .

Soon after I turned about in Fair Haven Pond it began to rain hard. The wind was but little south of east and therefore not very favorable for my voyage. I raised my sail and, cowering under my umbrella in the stern, wearing the umbrella like a cap and holding the handle between my knees, I steered and paddled, almost perfectly sheltered from the heavy rain. Yet my legs and arms were a little exposed sometimes, in my endeavors to keep well to windward so as to double certain capes ahead. For the wind occasionally drove me on to the western shore. From time to time from under my umbrella, I could see the ducks spinning away from me like great bees. For when they are flying low directly from you, you see hardly anything but their vanishing dark bodies, while the rapidly moving wings or paddles, seen edgewise, are almost invisible. At length when the river turned more easterly, I was obliged to take down my sail and paddle slowly in the face of the rain, for the most part not seeing my course, with the umbrella slanted before me. But though my progress was slow and laborious, and at length I began to get a little wet, I enjoyed the adventure because it combined to some extent the advantages of being at home in my chamber and abroad in the storm at the same time.

Fair again. To Great Sudbury Meadow by boat.

The river higher than before and rising. C. and I sail rap-

idly before a strong northerly wind—no need of rowing
upward, only of steering—cutting off great bends by crossing the meadows. We have to roll our boat over the road
at the stone bridge, Hubbard's causeway (to save the
wind), and at Pole Brook (to save distance).

It is worth the while to hear the surging of the waves
and their gurgling under the stern, and to feel the great
billows toss us, with their foaming yellowish crests. The
world is not aware what an extensive navigation is now
possible on our overflowed fresh meadows. It is more interesting and fuller of life than the sea bays and permanent
ponds. A dozen gulls are circling over Fair Haven Pond,
some very white beneath, with very long, narrow-pointed,
black-tipped wings, almost regular semicircles like the new
moon. As they circle beneath a white scud in this bright
air, they are almost invisible against it, they are so nearly
the same color. What glorious fliers! But few birds seen:
only a crow or two teetering along the water's edge looking
for its food, with its large clumsy head, and on unusually
long legs, as if stretched, or its pants pulled up to keep it
from the wet, and now flapping off with some large morsel
in its bill; or robins in the same place; or perhaps the sweet
song of the tree sparrows from the alders by the shore, or
of a song sparrow or blackbird. The phoebe is scarcely
heard. Not a duck do we see! . . .

We pause or lay to from time to time, in some warm
smooth lee, under the southwest side of a wood or hill.[5]

Sail to Ball's Hill.

The water is at its height, higher than before this year.
I see a few shad-flies on its surface. Scudding over the Great

---

[5] In New England a spring freshet is one of the events of that season.
In April, 1854, it rained steadily for three days, cleared for two days and
then rained again hard for two days more. The result was a regulation
spring freshet.

Meadows, I see the now red crescents of the red maples in their prime round about above the gray stems. The willow osiers require to be seen endwise the rows, to get an intense color. The clouds are handsome this afternoon: on the north some dark, windy clouds . . . but it is chiefly wind; southward, those summer clouds in numerous isles, light above and dark-barred beneath. Now the sun comes out and shines on the pine hill west of Ball's Hill, lighting up the light green pitch pines and the sand and russet-brown lichen-clad hill. That is a very New England landscape.

The water on the meadows is now quite high on account of the melting snow and rain. It makes a lively prospect when the wind blows, where our summer meads spread— a tumultuous sea, a myriad waves breaking with whitecaps, like gambolling sheep for want of other comparison in the country. Far and wide a sea of motion, schools of porpoises, lines of Vergil realized. One would think it a novel sight for inland meadows. Where the cranberry and andromeda and swamp white oak and maple grow, here is a mimic sea with its gulls. At the bottom of the sea—cranberries. . . .

I think our overflowing river far handsomer and more abounding in soft and beautiful contrasts than a merely broad river would be. A succession of bays it is, a chain of lakes, an endlessly scalloped shore, rounding wood and field. Cultivated field and wood and pasture and house are brought into ever new and unexpected positions and relations to the water. There is just stream enough for a flow of thought.

The strain of the red-wing on the willow spray over the water tonight is liquid, bubbling, watery, almost like a tinkling fountain, in perfect harmony with the meadow. It oozes, trickles, tinkles, bubbles from his throat—*bob-y-lee-e-e* —and then its shrill fine whistle.

The villagers walk the streets and talk of the great rise of waters.

I hear the greatest concerts of blackbirds—red-wings and crow blackbirds—nowadays, especially of the former. . . . The maples and willows along the river, and the button-bushes, are all alive with them. They look like a black fruit on the trees, distributed over the top at pretty equal distances. It is worth while to see how slyly they hide at the base of the thick and shaggy button-bushes at this stage of the water. They will suddenly cease their strains and flit away and secrete themselves low amid these bushes till you are past; or you scare up an unexpectedly large flock from such a place, where you had seen none.

I pass a large quire in full blast on the oaks etc., on the island in the meadow northwest of Peter's. Suddenly they are hushed, and I hear the loud rippling rush made by their wings as they dash away, and looking up, I see what I take to be a sharp-shinned hawk just alighting on the trees where they were, having failed to catch one. They retreat some forty rods off, to another tree, and renew their concert there. The hawk plumes himself, and then flies off, rising gradually and beginning to circle, and soon it joins its mate, and soars with it high in the sky and out of sight, as if the thought of so terrestrial a thing as a blackbird had never entered its head.

Coming out, I find it very warm, warmer than yesterday or any day yet. It is a reminisence of past summers. It is perfectly still and almost sultry, with wet-looking clouds hanging about, and from time to time hiding the sun. . . . And as I sit on Fair Haven Hill-side, the sun actually burns my cheek; yet I left some fire in the house, not knowing behind a window how warm it was. The flooded meadows and river are smooth, and just enough in shadow for reflections. The rush sparrows tinkle now at 3 P.M. far over the bushes, and hylodes are peeping in a distant pool. Robins are singing and peeping and jays are screaming. I see one or two smokes in the horizon. I can still see the mountains slightly spotted with snow. The frost is out enough for plowing probably in most open ground.

When I reach the top of the hill, I see suddenly all the southern horizon east or south from Bear Hill in Waltham to the river, full of a mist, like a dust, already concealing the Lincoln hills and producing distinct wreaths of vapor, the rest of the horizon being clear. Evidently a sea-turn, a wind from over the sea, condensing the moisture in our warm atmosphere and putting another aspect on the face of things. All this I see and say long before I feel the change, while still sweltering on the rocks, for the heat was oppressive. Nature cannot abide this sudden heat, but calls for her fan. In ten minutes I hear a susurrus in the shrub oak leaves at a distance, and soon an agreeable fresh air washes these warm rocks, and some mist surrounds me.[6]

The toads have begun fairly to ring at noonday in earnest. I rest awhile on my oars in this meadow amid the birches to hear them. . . . It is a low, terrene sound, the undertone of the breeze. Now it sounds low and indefinitely far, now rises, as if by general consent, to a higher key, as if in another and nearer quarter—a singular alternation. The now

---

[6] A sea-turn is a phrase common to the length of the New England coast. All that it implies is that a mass of air cooled by the ocean is now moving in over the land. The welcome change that it brings is particularly noticeable in that it is always abrupt and inclined to be sharp. The phrase is often on the lips of the down-east weather prophet as witness the testimony of Thoreau:

> I remember that the stage drivers riding back and forth daily from Concord to Boston and becoming weather wise perforce, often meeting the sea breeze on its way into the country, were wont to show their weather wisdom by telling anxious travellers that it was nothing but a sea-turn.

universal hard metallic ring of toads blended and partially drowned by the rippling wind. The voice of the toad, the herald of warmer weather.

Looking off on to the river meadow, I noticed, as I thought a stout stake aslant in the meadow, three or more rods off, sharp at the top and rather light-colored on one side, as is often the case; yet, at the same time, it occurred to me that a stake-driver often resembled a stake very much, but I thought, nevertheless, that there was no doubt about this being a stake. I took out my glass to look for ducks, and my companion, seeing what I had, and asking if it was not a stake-driver, I suffered my glass at last to rest on it, and I was much surprised to find that it was a stake-driver after all.

The bird stood in shallow water near a tussock, perfectly still, with its long bill pointed upwards in the same direction with its body and neck, so as perfectly to resemble a stake aslant. If the bill had made an angle with the neck it would have been betrayed at once. Its resource evidently was to rely on its form and color and immobility solely for its concealment. This was its instinct, whether it implies any conscious artifice or not. I watched it for fifteen minutes, and at length it relaxed its muscles and changed its attitude, and I observed a slight motion; and soon after, when I moved toward it, it flew.[7]

It is a pleasant sight, among the pleasantest, at this season, to see the at first reddish anthers of the sterile catkins of our earliest willow bursting forth on their upper sides like

---

[7] The American bittern, *Botaurus lentiginosus*, is frequently encountered in the *Journal*. This bird is known as the stake-driver because its call, as Thoreau noted "sounded exactly like a man pumping, while another man struck on the head of the pump with an axe, the last strokes sounding peculiarly dry and hard like a forcible echo from the woodside." It is this last that is so suggestive of the driving of a stake.

rays of sunshine from amidst the *downy* fog, turning a more and more lively yellow as the pollen appears—like a flash of sulphur. It is like the sun bursting out of a *downy* cloud or mists.

See on the water over the meadow, north of the boat's place, twenty rods from the nearest shore and twice as much from the opposite shore, a very large striped snake swimming. It swims with great ease, and lifts its head a foot above the water, darting its tongue at us. A snake thus met on the water appears far more monstrous, not to say aweful and venomous, than on the land. It is always something startling and memorable to meet with a serpent in the midst of a broad water, careering over it. But why had this one taken to the water? Is it possible that snakes ever hibernate in meadows which are subject to be overflown? This one when we approached swam toward the boat, apparently to rest on it, and when I put out my paddle, at once coiled itself partly around it and allowed itself to be taken on board. It did not hang down from the paddle like a dead snake, but stiffened and curved its body in a loose coil about it.

When I examine a flat sandy shore on which the ripples now break, I find the tracks of many little animals that have lately passed along it close to the water's edge. Some indeed have come out of the water and gone into it again. Minks, squirrels, and birds; they it is that walk these inland strands. The moist sand and mud which the water has but just ceased to dash over retains the most delicate impressions. . . . I now actually see one small-looking rusty or brown black mink scramble along the muddy shore and enter a hole in the bank.

Do not sail well till I reach Dove Rock, then glide swiftly up the stream. I move upward against the current with a moderate but fair wind, the waves somewhat larger, probably because the wind contends with the current. The sun is in my face, and the waves look particularly lively and sparkling. I can steer and write at the same time. They gurgle under my stern, in haste to fill the hollow which I have created. The waves seem to leap and roll like porpoises, with a slight surging sound when their crests break, and I feel an agreeable sense that I am swiftly gliding over and through them, bound on my own errands, while their motion is chiefly but an undulation, and an apparent one. It is pleasant, exhilarating, to feel the boat tossed up a little by them from time to time. Perhaps a wine drinker would say it was like the effect of wine. It is flattering to a sense of power to make the wayward wind our horse and sit with our hand on the tiller. Sailing is much like flying, and from the birth of our race men have been charmed by it.

I steer down straight through the Great Meadows, with the wind almost directly aft, feeling it more and more the farther I advance into them. They make a noble lake now. The boat, tossed up by the rolling billows, keeps falling again on the waves with a chucking sound which is inspiriting. There go a couple of ducks, which probably I have started, now scaling far away on motionless pinions, with a slight descent in their low flight, toward some new cove. Anon I scare up two black ducks which make one circle around me, reconnoitring and rising higher and higher then go down the river. Is it they that so commonly practice this manoeuvre? Peter's is now far behind me on a forgotten shore. The boat moored beneath his hill is no longer visible, and the red russet hill which is my goal rises before me. I moor my boat to a tree at the base of this hill.

The waves are breaking with violence on this shore as on a sea-beach, and here is the first painted tortoise just cast up by them and lying on his back amid the stones, in the most favorable position to display his bright-vermilion marks, as the waves still break over him.

What an entertainment this river affords! It is subject to so great overflows, owing to its broad intervals, that a day's rain produces a new landscape. Let it rain *heavily* one whole day, and the river will be increased from half a dozen rods in width to nearly a mile in some places, and, where I walked dry-shod yesterday a-maying, I sail with a smacking breeze today, and fancy that I am a sailor on the ocean. It is an advantage which all towns do not possess.

May

These days we begin to think in earnest of bathing in the river, and to sit at an open window. Life out of doors begins.

A.M.—To Battle-Ground by river. . . .
The flood on the meadows, still high, is quite smooth, and many are out this still and suddenly very warm morning, pushing about in boats. Now, thinks many a one, is the time to paddle or push gently far up or down the river, along the still, warm meadow's edge, and perhaps we may see some large turtles, or muskrats, or otter, or rare fish or fowl. It will be a grand forenoon for a cruise, to explore these meadow shores and inundated maple swamps which we have never explored. Now we shall be recompensed for the week's confinement to shop or garden. We will spend our Sabbath exploring these smooth warm vernal waters. Up

48

or down shall we go? To Fair Haven Bay and the Sudbury meadows [upstream] or to Ball's Hill and Carlisle Bridge [downstream]?

Along the meadow's edge, lined with willows and alders and maples, under the catkins of the early willow, and brushing those of the sweet-gale with our prow, where the sloping pasture and the ploughed ground submerged, are fast drinking up the flood. What fair isles, what remote coast shall we explore? What San Salvador or Bay of All Saints arrive at? All are tempted forth, like flies, into the sun. All isles seem fortunate and blessed today; all capes are of Good Hope. The same sun and calm that tempts the turtles out tempts the voyagers. It is an opportunity to explore their own natures, to float along their own shores. The woodpecker cackles and the crow blackbird utters his jarring chatter from the oaks and maples.

All well men and women who are not restrained by superstitious custom come abroad this morning by land or water, and such as have boats launch them and put forth in search of adventure. Others, less free, or it may be, less fortunate, take their station on bridges, watching the rush of water through them and the motions of the departing voyagers, and listening to the notes of blackbirds from over the smooth water. They see a swimming snake, or a muskrat dive—airing and sunning themselves there until the first bell rings.

The inhabitants of the river are peculiarly wide awake this warm day—fishes, frogs and toads, from time to time— and quite often I hear a tremendous rush of a pickerel after his prey. They are particularly active, maybe after the *Rana palustris,* now breeding. It is a perfect frog and toad day. I hear the stertorous notes of last evening from all sides of the river at intervals, but most from the grassiest and warmest or most sheltered and sunniest shores.

Walk to first stone bridge at sunset. . . . It is a glorious
evening. I scent the expanding willow leaves (for there are
very few blossoms yet) fifteen rods off. Already hear the
cheerful sprightly note of the yellowbird amid them. It is
perfectly warm and still, and the green grass reminds me
of June. The air is full of the fragrance of willow leaves.
The high water stretches smooth around. . . . The ring of
toads, the note of the yellowbird, the rich warble of the
red-wing, the thrasher on the hillside, the robin's evening
song, the woodpecker tapping some dead tree across the
water; and I see countless little fuzzy gnats in the air, and
dust over the road between me and the departed sun. . . .
Such an evening makes a crisis in the year. I must make
haste home and go out on the water.

I love to paddle now at evening when the water is smooth
and the air begins to be warm. The rich warble of blackbirds about retiring is loud and incessant, not to mention
the notes of numerous other birds. The black willow has
started but not yet the button-bush. Again I think I heard
the night warbler. Now, at starlight, that same nighthawk
or snipe squeak is heard, but no hovering. The first bat
goes suddenly zigzag overhead through the dusky air; comes
out of the dusk and disappears into it. That slumbrous snoring croak, far less ringing and musical than the toad's . . .,
now comes up from the meadow's edge. I save a floating
plank which exhales and imparts to my hands the rank scent
of the muskrats which have squatted on it. I often see their
fresh green excrement on rocks and wood. Already men
are fishing for pouts.

Moon not up. . . . The spearers are out, their flame a
bright yellow, reflected in the calm water. Without noise
it is slowly carried along the shores. It reminds me of the
light which Columbus saw on approaching the shores of

the New World. There goes a shooting star down towards
the horizon, like a rocket, appearing to describe a curve. . . .
The spearers' light reveals the forms of trees and bushes
near which it passes. When it is not seen, it makes a pillar
of reddish or rosy light on the twigs above it. I see even
the lamps of the village in the water, the river is so high.

The masses of the golden willow are seen in the distance
on either side of the way, twice as high as the road is wide,
conspicuous against the distant, still half-russet hills and
forests, for the green grass hardly yet prevails over the dead
stubble, and the woods are but just beginning to gray. . . .
At this season the traveller passes through a golden gate
on causeways where these willows are planted, as if he
were approaching the entrance to Fairyland; and there will
surely be found the yellowbird, and already from a distance
is heard his note, a *tche tche tche tcha tchar tcha*—ah willow, willow. . . . And as he passes between the portals, a
sweet fragrance is wafted to him; he not only breathes but
scents and tastes the air, and he hears the low humming
or susurrus of a myriad insects which are feeding on its
sweets. It is, apparently, these that attract the yellowbird.
The golden gates of the year, the *May*-gate.

Here on this causeway is the sweetest fragrance I have
perceived this season, blown from the newly flooded meadows. I cannot imagine what there is to produce it. No nose-
gay can equal it. It is ambrosially, nectareally, fine and
subtle, for you can see naught but the water, with green
spires of meadow grass rising above it. Yet no flower from
the Islands of the Blessed could smell sweeter. Yet I shall
never know whence it comes. Is it not all water-plants
combined? A fine, delicious fragrance, which will come to
the senses only when it will—willful as the gales.

The simple *peep peep* of the peetweet[1] as it flies away from the shore before me, sounds hollow and rather mournful, reminding me of the seashore and its wrecks, and when I smell the fresh odor of our marshes the resemblance is increased.

No tarts that I ever tasted at any table possessed such a refreshing, cheering, encouraging acid that literally put the heart in you and set you on edge for this world's experiences, bracing the spirit, as the cranberries I have plucked in the meadows in the spring. They cut the winter's phlegm, and now I can swallow another year of this world without any other sauce.

We are slow to realize water,—the beauty and magic of it. It is interestingly strange to us forever. . . .

When I got off this end of the Hollowell place I found myself in quite a sea with a smacking wind directly aft. I felt no little exhilaration, mingled with a slight awe, as I drove before this strong wind over the great black-backed waves I judged to be at least twenty inches or two feet high, cutting through them, and heard their surging and felt them toss me. I was even obliged to head across them and not get into their troughs, for then I could hardly keep my legs. They were crested with a dirty-white foam and were ten or twelve feet from crest to crest. They were so black, —as no sea I have seen,—large and powerful, and made such a roaring around me, that I could not but regard them as gambolling monsters of the deep. They were *melainai*— what is the Greek for waves?

This is our black sea. You see a *perfectly black* mass about two feet high and perhaps four or five feet thick and of indefinite length, round-backed, or perhaps forming a

---

[1] This is the familiar teeter-rail—the spotted sandpiper, *Actitis macularia*.

sharp ridge with a dirty-white crest, tumbling like a whale unceasingly before you. Only one of the epithets which the poets have applied to the color of the sea will apply to this water,—*melainia,* . . . I was delighted to find that our usually peaceful river could toss me so. How much more exciting than to be planting potatoes with those men in the field! What a different world!

The waves increased in height till [I] reached the bridge, the impulse of wind and waves increasing with the breadth of the sea. It is remarkable that it requires a very wide expanse to produce so great an undulation. The length of this meadow lake in the direction of the wind is about a mile, its breadth varying from a mile to a quarter of a mile, and the great commotion is toward the southerly end. Yet after passing the bridge I was surprised to find an almost smooth expanse as far as I could see, though the waves were about three inches high at fifty rods' distance. I lay awhile in that smooth water, and though I heard the waves lashing the other side of the causeway I could hardly realize what a sea I [had] just sailed through. It sounded like the breakers on the seashore heard from *terra firma.*

See a peetweet on Dove Rock, which just peeps out. As soon as the rocks begin to be bare the peetweet comes and is seen teetering on them and skimming away from me. Having fastened my boat at the maple, met, on the bank just above, Luke Dodge, whom I met in a boat fishing up that way once or twice last summer and previous years. Was surprised to hear him say,

"I am in my eighty-third year."

He still looks pretty strong and has a voice like a nutmeg-grater. Within two or three years at most, I have seen him walking, with that remarkable gait. It is encouraging to know that a man may fish and paddle in this river in his eighty-third year.

About 9 P.M. I went to the edge of the river to hear the
frogs. It was a warm and moist, rather foggy evening, and
the air was full of the ring of the toad, the peep of the
hylodes, and the low *growling* croak or stertoration of the
Rana palustris. Just there, however, I did not hear much of
the toad, but rather from the road, but I heard the steady
peeping of innumerable hylodes for a background to the
palustris snoring further over the meadow. There was a
universal snoring of the *R. palustris* all up and down the
river on each side, the very sounds that mine made in my
chamber last night,[2] and probably it began in earnest last
evening on the river. It is a hard, dry, unmusical, *fine* watch-
man's-rattle-like stertoration, swelling to a speedy conclusion
lasting some four or five seconds usually. . . .

I think that the different epochs in the revolution of the
seasons may perhaps be best marked by the notes of rep-
tiles. They express, as it were, the very feelings of the
earth or nature.

I hear in several places the low dumping notes of awak-
ened bullfrogs, what I call their *pebbly* notes, as if they
were cracking pebbles in their mouths; not the plump
dont dont or *ker dont*, but *kerdle dont dont*. As if they sat
around mumbling pebbles. At length near Ball's Hill, I
hear the first regular bullfrog's trump. . . . This sound,
heard low and far off over the meadows when the warmer
hours have come, grandly inaugurates the summer. . . . I

---

[2] On May 5, 1858, the *Journal* contains this curious entry:

> The two *Rana palustris* which I caught May 1st have been coupled
> ever since in a firkin in my chamber. They were not coupled when I
> caught them.

Thoreau elsewhere records that his Aunt Maria once asked him "to read
the life of Dr. Chalmers [The Rev. Thomas, D.D.] which however I did
not promise to do. Yesterday, Sunday, she was heard through the partition
shouting to my Aunt Jane, who is deaf:

> "Think of it! He stood half an hour today to hear the frogs croak,
> and he wouldn't read the life of Chalmers."

see three or four of them sitting silent in one warm meadow
bay. Evidently their breeding season now begins. But they
are soon silent as yet, and it is only an occasional and
transient trump that you hear. . . .

This note is like the first colored petals within the calyx
of a flower. It conducts us toward the germ of the flower
summer. He knows no winter. I hear in his tone the rumors
of summer heats. By this note he reassures the season. Not
till the air is of that quality that it can support this sound
does he emit it. It requires a certain sonorousness. The van
is lead by the croaking wood frog and the little peeping
hylodes, and at last comes this pursy trumpeter, the air
growing more and more genial, and even sultry, as well as
sonorous. . . . His trump is to the ear what the yellow lily
or spatter-dock is to the eye.

5.30 A.M.—To Nawshawtuct by river.

The first considerable fog I have noticed, at first as high
as the trees, curling gray over the water now beneath me,
as I paddle my boat, and through it I see the welling dimples
of the still stream. You are pretty sure now to hear the
stake-driver farther or nearer, morning or evening. Thought
I heard a tanager. . . . The fog has now risen up as high as
the houses at 6.15 and mingled with the smokes of the town.

Over meadows in boat at sunset to Island, etc.

The rain is over. There is a bow in the east. The earth
is refreshed; the grass is wet. The air is warm again and
still. The rain has smoothed the water to a glassy smoothness. It is very beautiful on the water now, the breadth of
the flood not yet essentially diminished. . . .

It is surprising what an electrifying effect this shower
appears to have had. It is like the christening of summer,
and I suspect that summer weather may be always ushered
in in a similar manner—thunder-shower, rainbow, smooth

water, and warm night. A rainbow on the brow of summer.
Nature has placed this gem on the brow of her daughter.
Not only the wet grass looks many shades greener in the
twilight, but the old pine needles also.

5.30 A.M.—To Island

The water is now tepid in the morning to the hands . . .
as I slip my hands down the paddle. Hear the wood pewee,
the warm-weather sound. As I was returning over the meadow this side of the Island, I saw the snout of a mud turtle
above the surface—little more than an inch of the point—and
paddled toward it. Then as he moved slowly on the surface,
different parts of his shell and head just appearing looked
just like the scalloped edges of some pads which had just
reached the surface. I pushed up and found a large snapping
turtle on the bottom.

He appeared of a dirty brown there, very nearly the color
of the bottom at present. With his great head, as big as an
infant's, and his vigilant eyes as he paddled about on the
bottom in his attempts to escape, he looked not merely
repulsive, but to some extent terrible even as a crocodile.
At length, after thrusting my arm in up to the shoulder
two or three times, I succeeded in getting him into the boat,
where I secured him with a lever under a seat. I could get
him from the landing to the house only by turning him
over and drawing him by the tail, the hard crests of which
afforded a good hold. For he was so heavy that I could not
hold him off so far as to prevent his snapping at my legs.
He weighed thirty and a half pounds. . . .

He had surprisingly stout hooked jaws, of a gray color
or bluish-gray, the upper shutting over the under, a more
or less sharp triangular beak corresponding to one below.
And his flippers were armed with very stout claws one and
a quarter inches long. He had a very ugly spiteful face with
a vigilant gray eye, which was never shut in any position

of the head, surrounded by the thick and ample folds of the skin about his neck. His shell was comparatively smooth and free from moss—a dirty black. He was a *dirty* or speckled white beneath.

He made the most remarkable and awkward appearance when walking. The edge of his shell was lifted about eight inches from the ground, tilting now to this side, then to that, his great scaly legs or flippers hanging with flesh and loose skin—slowly and gravely (?) hissing the while. His walking was perfectly elephantine. Thus he stalked along—a low conical mountain—dragging his tail, with his head turned upward with the ugliest and most venomous look, on his flippers, half leg half fin. But he did not proceed far before he sank down to rest. If he could support a world on his back when lying down, he certainly could not stand up under it. All said that he walked like an elephant.

When lying on his back, showing his *dirty* white and warty underside, with his tail curved round, he reminded you forcibly of pictures of the dragon. He could not easily turn himself back; tried many times in vain, resting betweenwhiles. Would inflate himself and convulsively spring with head and all upward, so as to lift his shell from the ground, and he would strike his head on the ground, lift up his shell, and catch at the earth with his claws. . . .

This then, is the season for hunting them, now that the water is warmer, before the pads are common, and the water is getting shallow on the meadows. E. Wood, Senior,[3] speaks of two seen fighting for a long time in the river in front of his house last year. I have heard of one being found

---

[3] "When I am behind Cheney's this warm and still afternoon, I hear a voice calling to oxen three quarters of a mile distant, and I know it to be Elijah Wood's. It is wonderful how far the *individual* proclaims himself Out of the thousand millions of human beings on this globe, I know that this sound was made by the lungs and larynx and lips of E. Wood, am as sure of it as if he nudged me with his elbow and shouted in my ear."— May 1, 1858.

in the meadow in the winter surrounded by frozen mud. Is not this the heaviest animal found wild in this township?

There is a surprising change since I last passed up the Assabet; the fields are now clothed with so dark and rich a green, and the wooded shore is all lit up with the tender, bright green of birches fluttering in the wind and shining in the light, and red maple keys are seen at a distance against the tender green of birches and other trees, tingeing them.

The wind is easterly, having changed, and produces an agreeable raw mistiness, unlike the dry blue haze of dog-days, just visible, between a dew and a fog for density. I sail up the stream, but the wind is hardly powerful enough to overcome the current, and sometimes I am almost at a standstill where the stream is most contracted and swiftest, and there I sit carelessly waiting for the struggle between wind and current to decide itself. Then comes a stronger puff, and I see by the shore that I am advancing to where the stream is broader and runs less swiftly and where lighter breezes can draw me. In contracted and swift-running places the wind and current are almost evenly matched. It is a pleasing delay, to be referred to the elements, and meanwhile I survey the shrubs on shore.

Standing in the meadow near the early aspen at the island, I hear the first fluttering of leaves—a peculiar sound at first unaccountable to me. The breeze causes the now fully expanded aspen leaves to rustle with a pattering sound, striking one another. It is much like a gentle surge breaking on a shore, or the rippling of waves. This is the first softer music which the wind draws from the forest, the woods generally being comparatively bare and just bursting into leaf. It was delicious to behold that dark mass and hear that soft rippling sound.

As we float down the river through the still and hazy air, enjoying the June-like warmth see the first king birds on the bare black willows with their broad white breasts and white-tipped tails; and the sound of the first bobolink was floated to us from over the meadows; now that the meadows are lit by the tender yellow green of the willows and the silvery-green fruit of the elms. . . . Some men are already fishing, indistinctly seen through the haze. . . .

The air is filled with the song of ₜbirds—warbling vireo, gold robin, yellowbirds, and occasionally the bobolink. The gold robin[4] just come, is heard in all parts of the village. I see both male and female. It is a remarkable difference between this day and yesterday, that yesterday this and the bobolink were not heard and now the former at least, is so musical and omnipresent. Even see boys a-bathing, though they must find it cold.

As I sat in my boat near the Bath Rock at Island, I saw a red squirrel steal slyly up a red maple, as if he were in search of a bird's nest . . . and I thought I would see what he was at. He crept far out on the slender branches, and, reaching out his neck, nibbled off the fruit stems, sometimes bending them in reach with his paw; and then, squatting on the twig, he voraciously devoured the half-grown keys, using his paws to direct them to his mouth as a nut. Bunch after bunch he plucked and ate, letting many fall, and he made an abundant if not sumptuous feast, the whole tree hanging red with fruit around him. It seemed like a fairy fruit as I sat looking toward the sun and saw the red keys made all glowing and transparent by the sun between me and the body of the squirrel. It was certainly a cheering sight, a cunning red squirrel perched on a slender twig be-

---

[4] The gold robin is an old-time Massachusetts name for the Baltimore oriole, *Icterus galbula*.

tween you and the sun, feasting on the handsome red
maple keys. He nibbled voraciously, as if they were a sweet
and lucious fruit to him. What an abundance and variety
of food is now ready for him! At length, when the wind
suddenly began to blow hard and shake the twig on which
he sat, he quickly ran down a dozen feet.

When yesterday Sophia and I were rowing past Mr.
Prichard's land, where the river is bordered by a row of
elms and low willows, at 6 P.M. we heard a singular note
of distress as it were from a catbird—a loud, vibrating, catbird sort of note, as if the cartbird's mew were imitated by
a smart vibrating spring. Blackbirds and others were flitting
about, apparently attracted by it. At first, thinking it was
merely some peevish catbird or red-wing, I was disregarding
it, but on second thought turned the bows toward the shore,
looking into the trees as well as over the shore, thinking
some bird might be in distress, caught by a snake or in a
forked twig. The hovering birds dispersed at my approach.
The note of distress sounded louder and nearer as I approached the shore covered with low osiers. The sound
came from the ground, not from the trees. I saw a little
black animal making haste to meet the boat under the osiers.
A young muskrat? a mink? No, it was a little dot of a kitten.
It was scarcely six inches long from the face to the base
—or I might as well say the tip—of the tail, for the latter
was a short sharp pyramid, perfectly perpendicular but not
swelled in the least. It was a very handsome and very precocious kitten, in perfectly good condition, its breadth being
considerably more than one third of its length. Leaving its
mewing, it came scrambling over the stones as fast as its
weak legs would permit, straight to me. I took it up and
dropped it into the boat, but while I was pushing off it ran
the length of the boat to Sophia, who held it while we
rowed homeward. Evidently it had not been weaned—was

smaller than we remembered that kittens ever were—almost infinitely small. Yet it had hailed a boat, its life being in danger, and saved itself. Its performance, considering its age and amount of experience, was more wonderful than that of any young mathematician or musician that I have read of.

Various were the conjectures as to how the kitten came there, a quarter of a mile from a house. The possible solutions were finally reduced to three. First, it must either have been born there, or, secondly, carried there by its mother, or, thirdly, by human hands. In the first case, it had possibly brothers and sisters, one or both, and its mother had left them to go a-hunting on her own account and might be expected back. In the second, she might equally be expected to return. At any rate, not having thought of all this till we got home, we found that we had got ourselves into a scrape. For this kitten, though exceedingly interesting, required one nurse to attend it constantly for the present, and, of course, another to spell the first. And, besides, we had already a cat well-nigh grown, who manifested such a disposition toward the young stranger that we had no doubt it would have torn it in pieces in a moment if left alone with it. As nobody made up his or her mind to have it drowned and still less to drown it, having once looked into its innocent extremely pale blue eyes—as of milk thrice skimmed—and had his finger or his chin sucked by it, while, its eyes being shut, its little paws played a soothing tune, it was resolved to keep it until it could be suitably disposed of.

It rested nowhere, in no lap, under no covert, but still faintly cried for its mother and its accustomed supper. It ran toward every sound or movement of a human being, and whoever crossed the room it was sure to follow at a rapid pace. It had all the ways of a cat of the maturest years; could purr divinely and raised its back to rub all boots and shoes. When it raised its foot to scratch its ear, which by the way it never hit, it was sure to fall over and roll on the floor. It climbed straight up the sitter, faintly mewing all the way, and sucked his chin. In vain, at first, its head was bent down into saucers of milk which its eyes did not see, and its chin was wetted. But soon it learned to suck a finger that had been dipped in it, and better still a rag; and then at last it slept and rested.

The street was explored in vain to find its owner and at length an Irish family took it into their cradle. Soon after we learned that a neighbor who had heard the mewing of kittens in the partition had sent for a carpenter, taken off a board, and found two the very day at noon that we sailed. That same hour it was first brought to the light a coarse Irish cook had volunteered to drown it, had carried it to the river, and without bag or sinker had cast it in! It saved itself and hailed a boat! What an eventful life! What a precocious kitten! We feared it owed its first plump condition to the water. How strong and effective the instinct of self-preservation!

Saw a greater telltale, and this, is the only one I have seen probably; distinguished by its size. It is very watchful, but not timid, allowing me to come quite near, while it stands on the lookout at the water's edge. It keeps nodding its head with an awkward jerk, and wades in the water to the middle of its yellow legs; goes off with a loud and sharp *phe phe phe phe,* or something like that. It acts the part of the telltale, though there are no birds here, as if [it] were with a flock. Remarkable as a sentinel for other birds.[5]

---

[5] The yellowleg is a large shore bird that walks upon stilted legs—one of the many sandpipers. There are two of them, the Lesser, *Totanus flavipes*—the Summer yellowleg—and the Greater, *Totanus melanoleucus*—the Winter yellowleg.

Fair Haven Lake now at 4.30 P.M. is perfectly smooth, reflecting the darker and glowing June clouds as it has not before. Fishes incessantly dimple it here and there, and I see afar, approaching steadily but diagonally toward the shore of the island, some creature on its surface, maybe a snake—but my glass shows it to be a muskrat, leaving two long harrow-like ripples behind. Soon after, I see another, quite across the Pond on the Baker Farm side, and even distinguish that to be a muskrat. The fishes, methinks are busily breeding now. These things I see as I sit on the top of Lee's Cliff, looking into the light and dark eye of the lake.

The heel of that summer-shower cloud, seen through the trees in the west, has extended further south and looks more threatening than ever. As I stand on the rocks, examining the blossoms of some forward black oaks which close over-hang it, I think I hear the sound of flies against my hat. No, it is scattered raindrops, though the sky is perfectly clear above me, and the cloud from which they come is yet far on one side. . . . But from the west a great, still, ash-colored cloud comes on.

The drops fall thicker and I seek a shelter under the Cliffs. I stand under a large projecting portion of the Cliff where there is ample space above and around, and I can move about as perfectly protected as under a shed. . . .

I sit at my ease and look out from under my lichen-clad rocky roof, half-way up the Cliff, under freshly leafing ash and hickory trees on to the pond, while the rain is falling faster and faster, and I am rather glad of the rain which affords me this experience. The rain has compelled me to find the cosiest and most homelike part of all the Cliff. The surface of the pond, though the rain dimples it all alike and I perceive no wind, is still divided into irregular darker and lighter spaces with distinct boundaries, as it were *watered* all over. Even now that it rains very hard and the surface is all darkened, the boundaries of those spaces are not quite obliterated. The countless drops seem to spring again from its surface like stalagmites. . . .

It lights up a little and the drops fall thinly again, and the birds begin to sing, but now I see a new shower coming up from the southwest, and the wind seems to have changed somewhat. Already I had heard the low mutterings of its thunder—for this is a thundershower—in the midst of the last. It seems to have shifted its quarters merely to attack me on a more exposed side of my castle. Two foes appear where I had expected none. But who can calculate the tactics of the storm?

It is a first regular summer thunder-shower, preceded by a rush of wind, and I begin to doubt if my quarters will prove a sufficient shelter. I am fairly besieged and know not when I shall escape. I hear the still roar of the rushing storm at a distance, though no trees are seen to wave. And now the forked flashes descending to the earth succeed rapidly to the hollow roars. above, and down comes the deluging rain. I hear the alarmed notes of birds flying to a shelter. The air at length is cool and chilly, the atmosphere is darkened, and I have forgotten the smooth pond and its reflections. The rock feels cold to my body, as if it were a different season of the year. I almost repent of having lingered here; think how far I should have got if I had started homeward. But then what a condition I should have been in! Who knows but the lightning will strike this cliff and topple the rocks down on me? The crashing thunder sounds like the overhauling of lumber on heaven's loft.

And now at last, after an hour of steady confinement, the clouds grow thin again, and the birds begin to sing. They make haste to conclude the day with their regular evening songs (before the rain is fairly over) according to their program. The pepe[6] on some pine tree top was heard almost in the midst of the storm. One or two bullfrogs trump. They care not how wet it is. Again I hear the still rushing, all-pervading roar of the withdrawing storm, when it is at least half a mile off, wholly beyond the pond, though no trees are seen to wave. It is simply the sound of the countless drops falling on the leaves and the ground. You were not aware what a sound the rain made. . . . My first stepping abroad seems but a signal for the rain to commence again. Not till after an hour and a half do I escape. After all, my feet and legs are drenched by the wet grass.[7]

Hundreds of swallows are now skimming close over the river, at its broadest part, where it is shallow and runs the swiftest, just below the Island, for a distance of twenty rods. They are bank, barn, cliff and chimney swallows all mingled together and continually scaling back and forth —a very lively sight. They keep descending or stooping to within a few inches of the water on a curving wing, without quite touching it, and I suppose are attracted by some small insects which hover close over it. They also stoop low about me as I stand on the flat island there, but I do not perceive the insects. They rarely rise more than five feet above the surface, and a general twittering adds to the impression of sociability.

May has been, on the whole, a pleasant month, with a few days of gentle rain-storm—fishermen's rains—straight down and spattering the earth.

---

[6] The olive-sided flycatcher.

[7] The next day Thoreau recorded: "—I sang 'Tom Bowling' there in the midst of the rain, and the dampness seemed to be favorable to my voice."

June

This is June, the month of grass and leaves. The deciduous trees are investing the evergreens and revealing how dark they are. Already the aspens are trembling again, and a new summer is offered me. I feel a little fluttered in my thoughts, as if I might be too late. Each season is but an infinitesimal point. It no sooner comes than it is gone. It has no duration. It simply gives a tone and hue to my thought. Each annual phenomenon is a reminiscence and prompting.

May is the bursting into leaf and early flowering, with much coolness and wet and a few decidedly warm days, ushering in summer; June, *verdure* and *growth* with not intolerable, but agreeable heat.

The light of June is not golden but silvery, not a torrid but somewhat temperate heat. See it reflected from the bent grass and the under sides of leaves. Also I perceive faint silvery gleaming ripples where there is a rapid in the river—from railroad bridge at Darby's—without sun on it.

P.M. Up Assabet. . . .
I look now from the yard to the waving and slightly glaucous-tinged June meadows edged by the cool shade—gelid—of shrubs and trees—a waving shore of shady bays and promontories—yet different from the August shades. It is beautiful and elysian. The air has now begun to be filled with a bluish haze. These virgin shades of the year, when everything is tender, fresh and green—how full of promise? promising bowers of shade in which heroes may repose themselves. I would fain be present at the birth of shadow. It takes place with the first expansion of the leaves.

I find sanicle just out on the Island. The black willows are already beautiful, and the hemlocks with their bead-work of new green. Are these not kingbird days, when, in clearer first June days full of light, this aerial, twittering bird flutters from willow to willow and swings on the twigs, showing his white-edged tail? . . .

When we returned to our boat at 7 P.M., I noticed first, to my surprise, that the river was all alive with leaping fish, their heads seen continually darted above water, and they were large fish too. Looking up I found that the whole atmosphere over the river was full of shad-flies. It was a *great flight of ephemerae.*

Two years later almost to a day and at the same time of the day—early evening—on the Assabet, Thoreau again watched the fish leaping for shad-flies.

The water was dimpled with the leaping fish. . . . At one place, against Dodge's Brook, where they were driven back by a strong head wind at a bend, more than usual were wrecked on the water and the fishes were leaping more numerously than elsewhere. The river was quite alive with them, and I had not thought there were so many in it— great black heads and tails continually thrust up on all sides of my boat. You had only to keep your eye on a floating fly a minute to see some fishy monster rise and swallow it with more or less skill and plashing. Some skillfully seized their prey without much plashing, rising in a low curve and just showing their backs; others rose up perpendicularly, half their length out of water, showing their black backs or white bellies or gleaming sides; others made a noisy rush at their prey and leaped entirely out of water, falling with a loud plash. You saw twenty black points at once. They seemed to be suckers; large fish, at any rate, and probably various kinds. What a sudden surfeit the fishes must have!

6:30 P.M.—On river, up Assabet, after the rain. . . .
As the light is obscured after sunset, the birds rapidly cease their songs, and the swallows cease to flit over the river. And soon the bats are seen taking the places of the swallows and flying back and forth like them, and commonly a kingbird will be heard twittering still in the air. After the bats, or half an hour after sunset, the water-bugs begin to spread themselves over the stream, though fifteen minutes earlier not one was seen without the pads—now, when it is difficult to see them or the dimples they make, except you look toward the reflected western sky. It is evident that they dare not come out thus by day for fear

of fishes, and probably the nocturnal or vespertinal fishes, as eels and pouts, do not touch them.

I hear the toad, which I have called "spray frog" falsely, *still*. He sits close to the edge of the water and is hard to find—hard to tell the direction though you may be within three feet. I detect him chiefly by the motion of the great swelling bubble in his throat. A peculiarly rich, sprayey dreamer, now at 2 P.M.! How serenely it ripples over the water! What a luxury life is to him! I have to use a little geometry to detect him. Am surprised at my discovery at last, while C. sits by incredulous.[1] Had turned our prow to shore to search. This rich, sprayey note possesses all the shore. It diffuses itself far and wide over the water and enters into every crevice of the noon, and you cannot tell whence it proceeds.

Boys are bathing at Hubbard's Bend, playing with a boat —I at the willows. The color of their bodies in the sun at a distance is pleasing, the not often seen flesh-color. I hear the sound of their sport borne over the water.

I desire to get wet and saturated with water. The North River, Assabet, by the old stone bridge affords the best bathing-place I think of—a pure sandy, uneven bottom— with a swift current, a grassy bank, and overhanging maples, with transparent water, deep enough, where you can see every fish in it. Though you stand still, you feel the rippling current about you.

---

[1] This was not the last time that Channing would have occasion to marvel at his companion's quick keen eyes. Three days later Thoreau recorded:

> I told C. to look into an old mortise-hole in Wood's Bridge for a white-bellied swallow's nest, as we were paddling under; but he laughed, incredulous. I insisted, and when he climbed up he scared out the bird. Five eggs.
> "You see the feathers about, do you not?
> "Yes," said he.

At 3 P.M., as I walked up the bank by the Hemlocks, I saw a painted tortoise just beginning its hole; then another a dozen rods from the river on the bare barren field near some pitch pines, where the earth was covered with cladonias, cinquefoil, sorrel, etc. Its hole was about two-thirds done. I stooped down over it, and to my surprise after a slight pause, it proceeded in its work, directly under and within eighteen inches of my face. I retained a constrained position for three quarters of an hour or more for fear of alarming it.

It rested on its fore legs, the front part of its shell about one inch higher than the rear, and this position was not changed essentially to the last. The hole was oval, broadest behind, about one inch wide and one and three quarters long, and the dirt already removed was quite wet or moistened. It made the hole and removed the dirt with its hind legs only, not using its tail or shell, which last of course could not enter the hole, though there was some dirt in it. It first scratched two or three times with one hind foot; then took up a pinch of the loose sand and deposited it directly behind that leg, pushing it backward to its full length and then deliberately opening it and letting the dirt fall; then the same with the other hind foot. This it did rapidly, using each leg alternately with perfect regularity, standing on the other one the while, and thus tilting up its shell each time, now to this side, then to that. There was half a minute or a minute between each change. The hole was made as deep as the feet could reach, or about two inches. It was very neat about its work, not scattering the dirt about any more than was necessary. The completing of the hole occupied perhaps five minutes.

It then without any pause drew its head completely into its shell, raised the rear a little, and protruded and dropped a wet flesh-colored egg into the hole, one end foremost, the red skin of its body being considerably protruded with it.

Then it put out its head again a little, slowly, and placed the egg at one side with one hind foot. After a delay of about two minutes it again drew in its head and dropped another and so on to the fifth—drawing in its head each time, and pausing somewhat longer between the last. The eggs were placed in the hole without any *particular* care—only well down and flat and [each] out of the way of the next—and I could plainly see them from above.

After these ten minutes or more, it without pause or turning began to scrape the moist earth into the hole with its hind legs, and when it had half filled it, it carefully pressed it down with the edges of its hind feet, dancing on them alternately, for some time, as on its knees, tilting from side to side, pressing by the whole weight of the rear of its shell. When it had drawn in thus all the earth that had been moistened, it stretched its hind legs further back and to each side, and drew in the dry and lichen-clad crust, and then danced upon and pressed that down, still not moving the rear of its shell more than one inch to right or left all the while, or changing the position of the forward part at all.

The thoroughness with which the covering was done was remarkable. It persevered in drawing in and dancing on the dry surface which had never been disturbed, long after you thought it had done its duty, but it never moved its fore feet, nor once looked round, nor saw the eggs it had laid. There were frequent pauses throughout the whole, when it rested, or ran out its head and looked about circumspectly, at any noise or motion. These pauses were especially long during the covering of its eggs, which occupied more than half an hour. Perhaps it was hard work.

When it had done, it immediately started for the river at a pretty rapid rate—the suddenness with which it made these transitions was amusing—pausing from time to time, and I judge that it would reach it in fifteen minutes. It was not easy to detect that the ground had been disturbed there.

An Indian could not have made his cache more skillfully. In a few minutes all traces of it would be lost to the eye.[2]

It suddenly began to rain with great violence, and we in haste drew up our boat on the Clamshell shore, upset it, and got under, sitting on the paddles, and so we were quite dry while our friends thought we were being wet to our skins. But we had as good a roof as they. It was very pleasant to lie there half an hour close to the edge of the water and see and hear the great drops patter on the river each making a great bubble; the rain seemed much heavier for it. The swallows at once and numerously began to fly low over the water in the rain, as they had not before, and the toads spray rang in it. After it began to hold up, the wind veered a little to the east and apparently blew back the rear of the cloud and blew a second rain somewhat in upon us.

As soon as the rain was over I crawled out, straightened my legs, and stumbled at once upon a little patch of strawberries within a rod—the sward red with them. These we plucked while the last drops were thinly falling.

To take shelter from the rain when out on the river often caused an entry in the Journal. *The undersides of the bridges particularly enthralled Thoreau, and elsewhere he has left one of those etched sentences that records his hankering for "the sub-pontean, the underbridge life."*

Rain again, and we take shelter under a bridge, and again under our boat, and again under a pine tree. It is worth

---

[2] On the following tenth of September Thoreau recorded that he could find no trace of the tortoise eggs, and he concluded that they must have been hatched. This was in 1855. In other years Thoreau kept careful track of the development of the eggs of tortoises and turtles, and with unerring accuracy opened their nests as the eggs were hatching.

the while to sit or lie through a shower thus under a bridge or under a boat on the bank, because the rain is a much more interesting and remarkable phenomenon under these circumstances. The surface of the stream betrays every drop from the first to the last, and all the variations of the storm, so much more expressive is the water than the comparatively brutish face of the earth. We no doubt often walk between drops of rain falling thinly, without knowing it, though if on the water we should have been advertised of it. At last the whole surface is nicked with the rebounding drops as if the surface rose in little cones to accompany or meet the drops, till it looks like the back of some spiny fruit or animal, and yet the different-colored currents, light and dark, are seen through it all; and then when it clears up, how gradually the surface of the water becomes more placid and bright, the dimples growing fewer and finer till the prolonged reflections of trees are seen in it, and the water is lit up with a joy which is in sympathy with our own, while the earth is comparatively dead.

The wind does not blow through our river valley just as the vanes indicate at home, but comformably to the form of the valley somewhat. It depends on whether you have a high and hilly shore to guide it, or a flat one which it may blow across. . . . As I was approaching Bittern Cliff, I had but little wind, but I said to myself, As soon as I reach the cliff I shall find myself in a current of wind blowing into the opening of the pond valley; and I did. Indeed, the wind blows through that part of the river valley above the water line somewhat as the water does below it.

I see from time to time a fish, scared by our sail, leap four to six feet through the air above the waves.

8 P.M.—Up North River to Nawshawtuct.

The moon full. Perhaps there is no more beautiful scene

than that on the North River seen from the rock this side
the hemlocks. As we look up-stream we see a crescent-
shaped lake completely embosomed in the forest. There is
nothing to be seen but the smooth black mirror of the water,
on which there is now the slightest discernible bluish mist,
a foot high, and thickset alders and willows and the green
woods without an interstice sloping steeply upward from its
very surface, like the sides of a bowl. The river is here
for half a mile completely shut in by the forest. One hemlock, which the current has undermined, has fallen over
till it lies parallel with the water, a foot or two above it
and reaching two thirds across the stream, its extremity
curving upward to the light, now dead. Here it has been for
a year or two, and it has only taken the place of others which
have successively fallen in and been carried away by the
stream. One lies now cast up on the shore. Some wild roses,
so pale now in the twilight that they look exactly like great
blackberry blossoms. I think *these* would look so at midday.

Saw a little skunk coming up the river-bank in the woods
at the White Oak, a funny little fellow, about six inches
long and nearly as broad. It faced me and actually compelled me to retreat before it for five minutes. Perhaps I
was between it and its hole. Its broad black tail, tipped
with white, was erect like a kitten's. It had what looked like
a broad white band drawn tight across its forehead or top-
head, from which two lines of white ran down, one on each
side of its back and there was a narrow white line down
its snout. It raised its back, sometimes ran a few feet forward, sometimes backward and repeatedly turned its tail
to me, prepared to discharge its fluid like the old. Such
was its instinct. And all the while it kept up a fine grunting
like a little pig or a squirrel. It reminded me that the red
squirrel, the wood-chuck and the skunk all make a similar
sound.

The stake-driver is at it in his favorite meadow. I followed the sound. At last I got within two rods, it seeming always to recede and drawing you like a will-o'-the-wisp further away into the meadows. When thus near, I heard some lower sounds at the beginning much more like striking on a stump or a stake, a dry hard sound; and then followed the gurgling, pumping notes, fit to come from a meadow. This was just within the blueberry and *Pyrus arbutifolia,* chokeberry bushes, and when the bird flew up alarmed I went to the place, but could see no water, which makes me doubt if water is necessary to it in making the sound. Perhaps it thrusts its bill so deep as to reach the water where it is dry on the surface. It sounds the more like wood-chopping or pumping, because you seem to hear the echo of the stroke or the reverse motion of the pump handle. . . .

After the warm weather has come, both morning and evening you hear the bittern pumping in the fens. It does not sound loud near at hand, and it is remarkable that it should be heard so far. Perhaps it is pitched on a favorable key. Is it not a call to its mate? Methinks that in the resemblance of this note to rural sounds, to sounds made by farmers, the protection, the security of the bird is designed. Minott[3] says:

"I call them belcher-squelchers. They go *slug-toot, slug-toot, slug-toot.*" . . .

Lying with my window open these warm, even sultry nights, I hear the sonorously musical trump of the bullfrogs from time to time, from some distant shore of the river, as if the world were given up to them. By those villagers who live on the street they are never seen and rarely heard

---

[3] George Minott was the "poetical farmer—who most realizes to me the poetry of a farmer's life." He lived across the road from Ralph Waldo Emerson, was a great storyteller and a source of many of the anecdotes and of the lore about Concord recorded in the *Journal.*

by day, but in the quiet sultry nights their notes ring from one end of the town to another. It is as if you had waked up in the infernal regions. I do not know for a time in what world I am.

June 15. . . . 8 P.M.—On River. . . .

It is candle light. The fishes leap. The meadows sparkle with the coppery light of fireflies. The evening star, multiplied by undulating water, is like bright sparks of fire continually ascending. The reflections of the trees are grandly indistinct. There is a low mist slightly enlarging the river, through which the arches of the stone bridge are just visible, as a vision. The mist is singularly bounded, collected here, while there is none there; close up to the bridge on one side and none on the other, depending apparently on currents of air. A dew in the air it is, which in time will wet you through. See stars reflected in the bottom of our boat, it being a quarter full of water. There is a low crescent of northern light and shooting stars from time to time. . . . Some dogs bay. A sultry night.

June 16. *Wednesday* 4.30 A.M.—A low fog on the meadows but not so much as last night—a low incense frosting them. The clouds scattered wisps in the sky, like a squadron thrown into disorder at the approach of the sun. The sun now gilds an eastern cloud a broad, bright, coppery-golden edge, fiery bright, notwithstanding which the protuberances of the cloud cast dark shadows ray-like up into the day. . . . There seems to have intervened no night. The heat of the day is unabated. You perspire before sunrise. The bullfrogs boom still. The river appears covered with an almost imperceptible blue film. The sun is not over the bank. What wealth in a stagnant river. There is music in every sound in the morning atmosphere. As I look up over the bay I see the reflections of the meadow woods and the Hosmer hill at a distance, the tops of the trees cut off by a slight ripple. Even the fine grasses on the near bank are distinctly reflected. Owing to the reflections of the distant woods and hills, you seem to be paddling into a vast hollow country, doubly novel and interesting. Thus the voyageur is lured onward to fresh pastures.

P.M. Up Assabet.

A thunder shower in the north. Will it strike us? How impressive this artillery of the heavens! It rises higher and higher. At length the thunder seems to roll quite across the sky and all round the horizon, even where there are no clouds, and I row homeward in haste. How by magic the skirts of the cloud are gathered about us, and it shoots forward over our head, and the rain comes at a time and place which baffles all our calculations! Just before it the swamp white oak in Merrick's pasture was a very beautiful sight, with its rich shade of green, its top as it were encrusted with light. Suddenly comes the gust, and the big drops slanting from the north, and the birds fly as if rudderless, and the trees bow and are wrenched. It comes against the windows like hail and is blown over the roofs like steam or smoke. It runs down the large elm at Holbrook's and shatters the house near by. It soon shines in silver puddles in the streets.

More thunder-showers threaten, and I can still trace those that are gone by. The fireflies in the meadows are very numerous, as if they had replenished their lights from the lightning. The far retreated thunder clouds low in the southeast horizon and in the north, emitting low flashes which reveal their forms, appear to lift their wings like fireflies; or it is a steady glare like the glow worm.

Summer

Is not June the month in which all trees and shrubs grow
—do far the greater part of their growing? Will the shoots
add much to their length in July?

The *Nymphaea odorata,* water nymph, sweet water-lily,
pond-lily, in bloom. A superb flower, our lotus, queen of
the waters. Now is the solstice in still waters. How sweet,
innocent, wholesome its fragrance! How pure its white
petals, though its root is in the mud! It must answer in my
mind for what the Orientals say of the lotus flower. . . .
We now have roses on the land and lilies in the water—
both land and water have done their best—now *just* after

the longest day. . . . The floral days. The red rose, with the intense color of many suns concentrated, spreads its tender petals perfectly fair, its flower not to be overlooked, modestly yet queenly on the edges of shade copses and meadows, against its green leaves, surrounded by blushing buds of perfect form; not only beautiful, but rightfully commanding attention; unspoiled by the admiration of gazers. And the water-lily floats on the smooth surface of slow waters, amid rounded shields of leaves, bucklers, red beneath, which simulate a green field, perfuming the air.

I have passed down the river before sunrise on a summer morning, between fields of lilies still shut in sleep; and when, at length, the flakes of sunlight from over the bank fell on the surface of the water, whole fields of white blossoms seemed to flash open before me, as I floated along, like the unfolding of a banner, so sensitive is this flower to the influence of the sun's rays.

It is pleasant to remember those quiet Sabbath mornings by remote stagnant rivers and ponds, when pure white water-lilies, just expanded, not yet infested by insects, float on the waveless water and perfume the atmosphere. Nature never appears more serene and innocent and fragrant. A hundred white lilies, open to the sun, rest on the surface smooth as oil amid their pads, while devil's-needles are glancing over them. It requires some skill so to pull a lily as to get a long stem. The great yellow lily, the spatterdock, expresses well the fertility of the river.

Is not this period more than any distinguished for flowers when roses, swamp-pinks, morning-glories, arethusas, pogonias, orchises, blue flags, epilobiums, mountain laurel, and white lilies are all in blossom at once?

See on the open grassy bank and shore, just this side of the Hemlocks, a partridge with her little brood. Being in my boat, I went within three rods, and they were hardly scared at all. The young were but little bigger than chickens four or five days old, yet could fly two or three rods. The partridge now takes out her brood to feed, all the country over; and what an extensive range they have—not confined to a barnyard.

In the little meadow pool, or bay, in Hubbard's shore, I see two old pouts tending their countless young close to the shore. The former are slate-colored. The latter are about half an inch long and very black, forming a dark mass from eight to twelve inches in diameter. The old are constantly circling around them—over and under and *through*—as if anxiously endeavoring to keep them together, from time to time moving off five or six feet to reconnoitre. The whole mass of the young—and there must be a thousand of them at least—is incessantly moving, pushing forward and stretching out. Are often in the form of a great pout, apparently keeping together by their own instinct chiefly, now on the bottom, now rising to the top. Alone they might be mistaken for pollywogs. The old, at any rate, do not appear to be very successful in their apparent efforts to communicate with and direct them. At length they break into four parts.

Saw a little pickerel with a minnow in his mouth. It was a beautiful little silver-colored minnow, two inches long, with a broad stripe down the middle. The pickerel held [it] crosswise near the tail, as he had seized it, and as I looked down on him, he worked the minnow along in his mouth toward the head, and then swallowed it head foremost. Was this instinct? Fishermen should consider this in giving form to their bait. The pickerel does not swallow

the bait at once, but first seizes it, then probably decides
how it can best be swallowed, and no doubt lets go again
in disgust some baits of which he can make neither head
nor tail.

To Billerica dam, surveying the bridges. . . .
The testimony of the farmers, etc., is that the river thirty
to fifty years ago was much lower in the summer than
now. . . . Ebenezer Conant remembers when the Canal dam
was built, and that before that it used to be dry at midsum-
mer outside the bushes on each side.

*Ebenezer Conant, then 81 years of age, was a great rec-
ollector—of the winter of the greatest snows and the like.
In June, 1859, when this entry occurs, Thoreau was em-
ployed for several days in surveying "the bridges and river
from Heard's Bridge to the Billerica dam." This latter, as
Ebenezer Conant's recollection gives evidence, had indubi-
tably been the cause of raising the level of the Concord
River and flowing out its extensive meadows. The dam had
been built to provide a head of water for the Middlesex
Canal which went into operation in 1803. This extensive
waterway, financed entirely by private funds, ran from
Middlesex Village just above Lowell on the Merrimack,
entering the Concord River at Billerica and then on to
Charlestown where access was had to Boston harbor.*

*Thereby the hinterland, known to old New Englanders
as "up-country," was tapped for the trade in what was then
called West India goods. The picturesque old canal tra-
versed the valleys in its course on aqueducts, and by means
of it and locks at the falls on the Merrimack, canal boats
traveled to and from Concord in New Hampshire and
Boston. The heyday of its operation was in the 1830's and
shortly thereafter it was eclipsed by the railroads.*

The story of the Middlesex Canal is a forgotten chapter in the history of American transportation. Remnants of this once formidable venture are still to be seen in the country-side of Middlesex County. And interestingly enough the dam at Billerica in thus backing up the flowage of the river, made the valley of the Concord a haven for wildlife as is evidenced by the present-day National Wildlife Refuge and the privately owned sanctuary in the Great Meadows. It was by the Middlesex Canal that Thoreau and his brother John reached the Merrimack on their river trip in 1839, as he recounted a decade later in the passage that follows in A Week on the Concord and Merrimack Rivers.

As we said before, the Concord is a dead stream, but its scenery is the more suggestive to the contemplative voyager, and this day its water was fuller of reflections than our pages even. Just before it reaches the falls in Billerica, it is contracted, and becomes swifter and shallower, with a yellow pebbly bottom, hardly passable for a canal-boat, leaving the broader and more stagnant portion above like a lake among the hills. All through the Concord, Bedford and Billerica meadows we had heard no murmur from its stream, except where some tributary runnel tumbled in.

But now at length we heard this staid and primitive river rushing to her fall, like any rill. We here left its channel, which runs, or rather is conducted, six miles through the woods to the Merrimack, at Middlesex; and as we did not care to loiter on this part of our voyage, while one ran along the tow-path drawing the boat by a cord, the other kept it off the shore with a pole, so that we accomplished the whole distance in little more than an hour. This canal, which is the oldest in the country, and has even an antique look beside the more modern railroads, is fed by the Concord, so that we were still floating on its familiar waters.

It is so much water which the river *lets* for the advantage
of commerce. There appeared some want of harmony in
its scenery, since it was not of equal date with the woods
and meadows through which it is led, and we missed the
conciliatory influence of time on land and water; but in
the lapse of ages, Nature will recover and endemnify herself, and gradually plant fit shrubs and flowers along its
borders. Already the kingfisher sat upon a pine over the
water, and the bream and pickerel swam below. Thus all
works pass directly out of the hands of the architect into
the hands of Nature, to be perfected.

It was a retired and pleasant route, without houses or
travelers, except some young men who were lounging upon
a bridge at Chelmsford. . . .

The river meadows on each side of the stream, looking
toward the light, have an elysian beauty. A light yellow
plush or velvet, as if some gamboge had been rubbed into
them. They are by far the most bright and sunny-looking
spots, such is the color of the sedges which grow there,
while the pastures, and hillsides are dark green and the
grain fields glaucous green. It is remarkable that the meadows which are the lowest part, should have this lightest,
sunniest, yellowest look.

I see the smooth river in the north reflecting two shades
of light, one from the water, another from the surface of
the pads which broadly border it on both sides, and the
very irregular waving or winding edge of the pads, especially perceptible in this light, makes a very agreeable
border to distinguish—the edge of the film which seeks
to bridge over and inclose the river wholly. These pads are
to the smooth water between like a calyx to its flower. The
river at such an hour, seen half a mile away, perfectly smooth
and lighter than the sky, reflecting the clouds, is a paradisai-

cal scene. What are the rivers around Damascus to this river sleeping around Concord? Are not the Musketaquid and the Assabet, rivers of Concord, fairer than the rivers of the plain?

June is an up-country month, when our air and landscape is most like that of a more mountainous region, full of freshness, with the scent of ferns by the wayside.

July

Methinks our warm weather hardest to bear is the last half of June and the first half of July. Afterward the shade and the dog-days give us moisture and coolness, especially at night.

I looked down on the river behind Dodd's at 2.30 P.M., a slate-colored stream with a scarcely perceptible current, with a male and female shore; the former, more abrupt, of button-bushes and willows, the other, flat, of grass and pickerel weed alone. Beyond the former, the water being deep, extends a border or fringe of green and purplish pads lying perfectly flat on the surface, but on the latter side the pads extend a half a rod or a rod beyond the pickerel-weed —shining pads reflecting the light, dotted with white or yellow lilies. This sort of ruff does the river wear, and so the land is graduated off to water.

A tender place in Nature, an exposed vein, and Nature making a feint to bridge it quite over with a paddy film, with red-winged blackbirds liquidly warbling and whistling in the willows, and the kingbirds on the elms and oaks; these pads, if there is any wind, rippling with the water and helping to smooth and allay it. It looks tender and exposed, as if it were naturally subterranean, and now, with these shields of pads, held scale-like by long threads from the bottom, she makes a feint to bridge it. So floats the Musketaquid over its segment of the sphere.

The river, too, steadily yields its crop. In louring days it is remarkable how many villagers resort to it. It is of more worth than many gardens. I meet one, late in the afternoon, going to the river with his basket on his arm and his pole in hand, not ambitious to catch pickerel this time, but he thinks he may perhaps get a mess of small fish. These [sic] kind of values are real and important, though but little appreciated, and he is not a wise legislator who underrates them and allows the bridges to be built low so as to prevent the passage of small boats. The town is but little conscious how much interest it has in the river, and might vote it away any day thoughtlessly. There is always to be seen either some unshaven wading man, an old mower of the river meadows, familiar with waters, vibrating his long pole over the lagoons of the off-shore pads, or else some solitary fisher, in a boat behind the willows, like a mote in the sunbeams reflecting the light; and who can tell how many a mess of river fish is daily cooked in the town? They are an important article of food to many a poor family.

July 1 [1852] . . . The white lilies were in all their splendor, fully open, sometimes their lower petals lying flat on the surface. The largest appeared to grow in the shallower water, where some stood five or six inches out of water, and were five inches in diameter. Two which I examined had twenty-nine petals each. We pushed our boat into the

midst of some shallow bays, where the water, not more
than a foot deep, was covered with pads and spotted white
with many hundreds of lilies which had just expanded. Yet
perhaps there was not one open which had not an insect
in it, and most had some hundreds of small gnats, which,
however, we shook out without much trouble, instead of
drowning them out, which makes the petals close.

The freshly opened lilies were a pearly white, and though
the water amid the pads was quite unrippled, the passing
air gave a slight oscillating, boat-like motion to and fro to
the flowers, like boats held fast by their cables. Some of the
lilies had a beautiful rosaceous tinge, most conspicuous in
the half-opened flower, extending through the calyx to the
second row of petals, on those parts of the petals between
the calyx-leaves which were most exposed to the influence
of the light. They were tinged with red, as they are very
commonly tinged with green, as if there were a gradual
transition from the stamens to the petals. It seemed to be
referred to the same coloring principle which is seen in the
under sides of the pads as well as the calyx-leaves. Yet
these rosaceous ones are chiefly interesting to me for variety, and I am contented that lilies should be white and
leave those higher colors to the land.

I wished to breathe the atmosphere of lilies, and get
the full impression which lilies are fitted to make. The form
of this flower is also very perfect, the petals are so distinctly
arranged at equal intervals and at all angles, from nearly
a perpendicular to horizontal about the centre. And buds
that were half expanded were interesting, showing the
regularly notched outline of the points of the petals above
the erect green calyx-leaves.

Some of these bays contained a quarter of an acre,
through which we with difficulty forced our boat. . . .

After eating our luncheon at Rice's Landing, we observed
that every white lily in the river was shut—and they re-

mained so all the afternoon, though it was no more sunny nor cloudy than the forenoon—except some which I had plucked before noon and cast into the river, which, floating down, lodged amid the pondweed, which continued fresh but had not the power to close their petals. It would be interesting to observe how instantaneously these lilies close at noon. I only observed that, though there were myriads fully open before I ate my lunch at noon, after dinner I could not find one open anywhere for the rest of the day.

I will here [July 4, 1852] tell the history of my rosaceous lilies plucked the first of July. They were buds at the bottom of a pitcher of water all the 2nd, having been kept in my hat[1] part of the day before. On the morning of the third I assisted their opening, and put them in water, as I have described; but they did not shut up at noon, like those in the river, but at dark, their petals, at least, quite tight and close. They all opened again in the course of the forenoon of the 4th, but had not shut up at 10 o'clock P.M., though I found them shut in the morning of the fifth. May it be that they can bear only a certain amount of light, and these being in the shade, remained open longer? I think not, for they shut up in the river that quite cloudy day, July 1st. Or is their vitality too little to permit [them] to perform their regular functions?

I have plucked a white lily bud just ready to expand, and, after keeping it in water for two days, have turned

---

[1] Ten days before on June 23d, Thoreau had recorded:

I am inclined to think that my hat, whose lining is gathered in midway so as to make a shelf, is about as good a botany-box as I could have and far more convenient, and there is something in the darkness and the vapors that rise from the head—at least if you take a bath—which preserves flowers through a long walk. Flowers will frequently come fresh out of this botany-box at the end of the day, though they have had no sprinkling.

back its sepals with my hand and touched the lapped
points of the petals, when they sprang open and rapidly
expanded in my hand into a perfect blossom, with the
petals as perfectly disposed at equal intervals as on their
native lakes, and in this case, of course, untouched by any
insect. I cut its stem short and placed it in a broad dish of
water, where it sailed about under the breath of the be-
holder with a slight undulatory motion. The breeze of his
half-suppressed admiration it was that filled its sail. It was
a rare-tinted one. A kind of popular aura that may be
trusted methinks. Men will travel to the Nile to see the
lotus flower, who have never seen in their glory, the lotuses
of their native streams.

The rich crimson undersides—with their regularly branch-
ing veins—of some white lily pads surpasses the color of
most flowers. No wonder the spiders are red that swim beneath; and think of the fishes that swim beneath this
crimson canopy—beneath a crimson sky. I can frequently
trace the passage of a boat, a pickerel fisher, perhaps, by
the crimson under sides of the pads upturned.

At the bathing place [Hubbard's] there is [a] hummock
which was floated on to the meadow some springs ago, now
densely covered with the handsome red-stemmed wild rose,
a full but irregular clump, from the ground, showing no
bare stems below, but a dense mass of shining leaves and
small red stems above in their midst, and on every side
now, in the twilight, more than usually beautiful they appear. Countless roses, partly closed, of a very deep rich
color, as if the rays of the departed sun still shone through
them; a more spiritual rose at this hour, beautifully blushing; and then the unspeakable beauty and promise of those
fair swollen buds that spot the mass, which will blossom
tomorrow, and the more distant promise of the handsomely

formed green ones, which yet show no red, for few things
are handsomer than a rosebud in any stage; these mingled
with a few pure white elder blossoms and some rosaceous
or pinkish meadow-sweet heads. I am confident that there
can be nothing so beautiful in any cultivated garden, with
all their varieties, as this wild clump.

As you walk beside a ditch or brook, you see the frogs
which you alarm launching themselves from a considerable
distance into the brook. They spring considerably upward,
so as to clear all intervening obstacles and seem to know
pretty well where the brook is. Yet no doubt they often
strike, to their chagrin and perhaps sorrow, on a pebbly
shore or rock. Their noses must be peculiarly organized to
resist accidents of this kind, and allow them to cast themselves thus heedlessly into the air, trusting to fall into the
water, for they come down nose foremost. A frog reckons
that he knows where the brook is. I shudder for them when
I see their soft, unshielded proboscis falling thus heedlessly
on whatever may be beneath.

P.M.—Down river in boat to the Holt. . . .
It is perhaps the warmest day yet. We hold on to the
abutments under the red bridge to cool ourselves in the
shade. No better place in hot weather, the river rippling
away beneath you and the air rippling through beneath the
abutments, if only in sympathy with the river, while the
planks afford a shade, and you hear all the travel and the
travellers' talk without being seen or suspected. The bullfrog it is, methinks, that makes the dumping sound. There
is generally a current of air circulating over water, always,
methinks, if the water runs swiftly, as if it put the air in
motion. There is quite a breeze here this sultry day. Com-
mend me to the sub-pontean, the under-bridge life.

The red lily, with its torrid color and sun-freckled spots, dispensing too with the outer garment of a calyx, its petals so open and wide apart that you can see through it in every direction, tells of hot weather. It is a handsome bell shape, so upright, and the *flower* prevails over every other part. . . .

Bathing is an undescribed luxury. To feel the wind blow on your body, the water flow on you and lave you, is a rare physical enjoyment this hot day. The water is remarkably warm here—especially in the shallows—warm to the hand, like that which has stood long in a kettle over a fire. The pond water being so warm made the water of the brook feel very cold; and this kept close on the bottom of the pond for a good many rods about the mouth of the brook, as I could feel with my feet; and when I thrust my arm down where it was only two feet deep, my arm was in the warm water of the pond, but my hand in the cold water of the brook.

2 P.M.—To the Assabet. . . .

Divesting yourself of all clothing but your shirt and hat, which are to protect your exposed parts from the sun, you are prepared for the fluvial excursion. You choose what depths you like, tucking your toga higher or lower, as you take the deep middle of the road or the shallow sidewalks. Here is a road where no dust was ever known, no intolerable drouth. Now your feet expand on a smooth sandy bottom, now contract timidly on pebbles, now slump in genial fatty mud—greasy, saponaceous—amid the pads. You scare out whole schools of small breams and perch, and sometimes a pickerel, which have taken shelter from the sun under the pads. This river is so clear compared with the South Branch or main stream, that all their secrets are betrayed to you.

Or you meet with and interrupt a turtle taking a more leisurely walk up the stream. Ever and anon you cross some furrow in the sand, made by a muskrat, leading off to right or left to their galleries in the bank, and you thrust your foot into the entrance, which is just below the surface of the water and is strewn with grass and rushes, of which they make their nests. In shallow water near the shore, your feet at once detect the presence of springs in the bank emptying in, by the sudden coolness of the water, and there, if you are thirsty, you dig a little well in the sand with your hands, and when you return, after it has settled and clarified itself, get a draught of pure cold water there.

I wonder if any Roman emperor ever indulged in such luxury as this—of walking up and down a river in torrid weather with only a hat to shade the head. What were the baths of Caracalla to this? Now we traverse a long water plain some two feet deep; now we descend into a darker river valley, where the bottom is lost sight of and the water rises to our armpits; now we go over a hard iron pan; now we stoop and go under a low bow of the *Salix nigra;* now we slump into soft mud amid the pads of the *Nymphoea odorata* [water lilies], at this hour shut. On this road there is no other traveller to turn out for.

Observed a pickerel in the Assabet, about a foot long, headed upstream, quasi-transparent (such its color) with darker and lighter parts contrasted, very still while I float quite near. There is a constant motion of the pectoral fins and also a waving motion of the ventrals, apparently to resist the stream, and a slight waving of the anal, apparently to preserve its direction. It darted off at last by a strong sculling motion of its tail.

The river is now so low that you can see its bottom, shined on by the sun, and travellers stop to look at fishes as they go over, leaning on the rails. The pickerel weed sends up its heavenly blue.

Bathed at Clamshell. See great schools of minnows, apparently shiners, hovering in the clear shallow next the shore. They seem to choose such places for security. They take pretty good care of themselves and are harder to catch with the hands than you expect, darting out of the way at last quite swiftly. Caught three, however, between my hands. They have brighter golden irides, all the abdomen conspicuously pale-golden, the back and half down the sides pale-brown, a broad, distinct black band along sides —which methinks marks the shiner—and comparatively transparent beneath behind vent. When the water is gone I am surprised to see how they can skip or spring from side to side in my cup-shaped two hands for a long time. This is to enable them to get off floating planks or pads on the shore when in fright they may have leaped on to them. But they are very tender and the sun and air soon kill them. If there is any water in your hand they will pass out through the smallest crack between your fingers.

How far behind the spring seems now—farther off perhaps, than ever, for this heat and dryness is most opposed to spring. Where most I sought for flowers in April and May I do not think to go now; it is either drought and barrenness or fall there now. The reign of moisture is long over. For a long time the year feels the influence of the snows of winter and the long rains of spring, but now how changed. It is like another and a fabulous age to look back on, when earth's veins were full of moisture, and violets burst out on every hillside. Spring is the reign of water; summer of heat and dryness; winter of cold. Whole families of plants that lately flourished have disappeared. Now the phenomena are tropical. Let our summer last long enough, and our

land would wear the aspect of the tropics. The luxuriant
foliage and growth of all kinds shades the earth and is
converting every copse into a jungle. Vegetation is rampant.
There is not such rapid growth, it is true, but it slumbers
like a serpent that has swallowed its prey. Summer is one
long drought. Rain is the exception.

I see at 9.30 P.M. a little brood of four or five barn swallows, which have quite recently left the nest, perched close
together for the night on a dead willow twig in the shade
of the tree, about four feet above the water. Their tails
not yet much grown. When I passed up, the old bird
twittered about them in alarm. I now float within four feet,
and they do not move or give sign of awaking. I could
take them all off with my hand. They have been hatched
in the nearest barn or elsewhere, and have been led at
once to roost here, for coolness and security. There is no
cooler nor safer place for them. I observe that they take
their broods to the telegraph wire for an aerial perch, where
they teach them to fly.

As we push away from Monroe's shore [en route to the
Sudbury meadows in his boat], the robins are singing and
the swallows twittering. There is hardly a cloud in the sky.
There are dewy cobwebs on the grass; so this is a fit morning for any adventure. It is one of those everlasting mornings . . . which are provided for long enterprises. It is a
sabbath within the water as well as in the air and on the
land, and even the little pickerels not half so long as your
finger appear to be keeping it holy amid the pads. There is
a sort of dusty or mealy light in the bream's tail and fins
waving in clear water. The river is now in its glory, adorned
with water lilies on both sides. . . .
We are gliding swiftly up the river by Barrett's Bend.
The surface of the water is the place to see pontederia

from, for now the spikes of flowers are all brought into a dense line—a heavy line of blue, a foot or more in width, on one or both sides of the river. . . . We take a bath at Hubbard's Bend. The water seems fresher, as the air, in the morning. Again under weigh, we scare up the great bittern amid the pontederia, and, rowing to where he alights come within three feet of him and scare him up again. He flies sluggishly away ploughing the air with the coulter of his breast-bone, and alighting ever higher up the stream. We scare him up many times in the course of an hour. The surface of the river is spotted with the radical leaves of the floating-heart, large and thin and torn, rarely whole, which something has loosened from the bottom. The larks and blackbirds and kingbirds are heard in the meadows. But few button-bushes are in blossom yet. Are they dark-brown weed-like fibrous roots of the plant itself that invest its stems below? Harmless bright downy clouds form in the atmosphere on every side and sail the heavens.

After passing Hubbard's Bridge, looking up the smooth river between the rows of button-bushes, willows and pads, we see the sun shining on Fair Haven Hill behind a sun-born cloud, while we are in shadow—a misty, golden light, yellow, fern-like, with shadows of clouds flitting across its slope—and horses in their pasture standing with outstretched necks to watch us; and now they dash up the steep in single file, as if to exhibit their limbs and mettle. The carcass of a cow which has recently died lies on the sandy shore under Fair Haven, close to the water. Perhaps she was poisoned with the water parsnip, which is now in flower and abounds along the side of the river.

We have left the dog in the middle of Fair Haven Bay, swimming in our wake, while we are rowing past Lee's, and we see no more of him. How simple are the ornaments of a farmhouse! To one rowing past in the middle of a warm summer day, a well at a distance from the house in the shadow of an oak, as here, is a charming sight. The house, too, with no yard but an open lawn sloping to the river. And young turkeys seen wandering in the grass, and ever and anon hopping up as if a snake had scared them. The pontedarias are alive with butterflies. Here is a fisherman's willow pole left to mark a lucky place, with green shoots at the top. . . .

No one has ever put into words what the odor of water-lilies expresses. A sweet and innocent purity. The perfect purity of the flower is not to be surpassed. They now begin to shut up. Looking toward the sun, I cannot see them, cannot distinguish lilies from the sun reflected from the pads.

Thus we go on, into the Sudbury meadows, opening the hills. . . .

When near home, just before sundown, the sun still inconveniently warm, we were surprised to observe on the uppermost point of each pontederia leaf a clear drop of dew already formed, or flowing down the leaf, where all seemed warmth and dryness, also as often hanging from the lobes below. It appeared a wonderful chemistry by which the broad leaf had collected this pearly drop on its uppermost extremity. The sun had no sooner sunk behind the willows and the button-bushes, than this process commenced. And now we see a slight steam like smoke rising from amidst the pontederias. In half an hour the river and the meadows are white with fog, like a frosted cake. As you stand on the bank in the twilight, it suddenly moves up in sprayey clouds, moved by an unfelt wind, and invests you where you stand, its battalions of mists reaching even to the road.

We have very few bass trees in Concord, but walk near them at this season and they will be betrayed, though several rods off, by the wonderful susurrus of the bees, etc., which their flowers attract. . . . I was warned that I was

passing one in two instances on the river—the only two
I passed—by this remarkable sound. At a little distance
[it] is like the sound of a waterfall or of the cars; close at
hand like a factory full of looms. They were chiefly bum-
blebees, and the great globose tree was all alive with them.

5 P.M. Up Assabet.

As I was bathing under the swamp white oaks at 6 P.M.,
heard a suppressed sound often repeated, like, perhaps the
working of beer through a bung-hole, which I already suspected to [be] produced by owls. I was uncertain whether
it was far or near. Proceeding a dozen rods up-stream on
the south side, toward where a catbird was incessantly
mewing, I found myself suddenly within a rod of a gray
screech owl sitting on an alder bough with horns erect,
turning its head from side to side and up and down, and
peering at me in that same ludicrously solemn and complacent way that I had noticed in one in captivity. Another, more red, also horned repeated the same warning
sound, or apparently call to its young, about the same distance off, in another direction, on an alder.

When they took to flight they made some noise with
their wings. With their short tails and squat figures they
looked very clumsy, all head and shoulders. Hearing a fluttering under the alders, I drew near and found a young
owl, a third smaller than the old, all gray, without obvious
horns, only four or five feet distant. It flitted along two
rods, and I followed it. I saw at least two more young. All
this was close by that thick hemlock grove and they perched
on alders, and an apple tree in the thicket there. These
birds kept opening their eyes when I moved, as if to get
clearer sight of me. The young were very quick to notice
any motion of the old, and so betrayed their return by
looking in that direction when they returned, though I
had not heard it. Though they permitted me to come so

near with so much noise, as if bereft of half their senses, they at [once] noticed the coming and going of the old birds, even when I did not. There were four or five owls in all.

4 A.M. To Cliffs.

This early twitter or breathing of chip-birds in the dawn sounds like something organic in the earth. This is a morning celebrated by birds. Our bluebird sits on the peak of the house and warbles as in the spring, but as he does not now by day. This morning is all the more glorious for a white fog, which, though not universal, is still very extensive over all lowlands, some fifty feet high or more, though there was none at ten last night. There are white cobwebs on the grass. The battalions of the fog are continually on the move. . . .

From Fair Haven Hill, the sun having risen, I see great wreaths of fog far northeast, revealing the course of the river, a noble sight, as it were the river elevated, or rather the ghost of the ample stream that once flowed to ocean between these now distant uplands in another geological period, filling the broad meadows—the dews saved to the earth by this great Musketaquid, condenser, refrigerator. And now the rising sun makes glow with downiest white the ample wreaths, which rise higher than the highest trees. The farmers that lie slumbering on this their day of rest, how little do they know of this stupendous pageant! The bright, fresh aspect of the woods glistening with moisture when the early sun falls on them.

As I came along, the whole earth resounded with the crowing of cocks, from the eastern unto the western horizon, and as I passed a yard, I saw a white rooster on the topmost rail of a fence pouring forth his challenges for destiny to come on. This salutation was traveling round the world; some six hours since had resounded through England,

France, and Spain; then the sun passed over a belt of silence where the Atlantic flows, except a clarion here and there from some cooped-up cock upon the waves, till greeted with a general all-hail along the Atlantic shore.

Looking now from the rocks, the fog is a perfect sea over the great Sudbury meadows in the southwest, commencing at the base of this Cliff and reaching to the hills south of Wayland, and further still to Framingham, through which only the tops of the higher hills are seen as islands, great bays of the sea, many miles across, where the largest fleets would find ample room and in which countless farms and farmhouses are immersed. The fog rises highest over the channel of the river and over the ponds in the woods which are thus revealed. I clearly distinguish where White Pond lies by this sign, and various other ponds, methinks, to which I have walked ten or twelve miles distant, and I distinguish the course of the Assabet far in the west and southwest beyond the woods. Every valley is densely packed with downy vapor. What leveling on a great scale is done thus for the eye! The fog rises to the top of Round Hill in the Sudbury meadows, whose sunburnt yellow grass makes it look like like a low sand-bar in the ocean, and I can judge thus pretty accurately what hills are higher than this by their elevation above the surface of the fog.

Every meadow and watercourse makes an arm of this bay. The primeval banks make thus a channel which only the fogs of late summer and autumn fill. The Wayland hills make a sort of promontory or peninsula like some Nahant. As I look across thither, I think of the sea monsters that swim in that sea and of the wrecks that strew the bottom, many fathoms deep, where, in an hour, when this sea dries up, farms will smile and farmhouses be revealed. A certain thrilling vastness or wasteness it now suggests. This is one of those ambrosial, white, ever-memorable fogs presaging fair weather. It produces the most picturesque and grandest effects as it rises, and travels hither and thither, enveloping and concealing trees and forests and hills. It is lifted up now into quite a little white mountain over Fair Haven Bay, and, even on its skirts, only the tops of the highest pines are seen above it, and all adown the river it has an uneven outline like a rugged mountain ridge; in one place some rainbow tints, and far, far in the south horizon, near the further verge of the sea (over Saxonville?) it is heaved up into great waves, as if there were breakers there.

In the meanwhile the wood thrush and the jay and the robin sing around me here, and birds are heard singing from the midst of the fog. And in one short hour this sea will all evaporate and the sun will be reflected from farm windows on its green bottom.

On Fair Haven a quarter of an hour before sunset. . . .
A golden sheen is reflected from the river so brightly that it dazzles me as much as the sun. The now silver-plated river is burnished gold there, and in the midst of all I see a boat ascending with regular dip of its seemingly gilt oars. That which appears a strip of smooth, light silvery water on each side of the stream, not reflecting the sky, is the reflection of light from the pads. From their edges, there stream into the smooth channel sharp blue serrations or ripples of various lengths, sometimes nearly across, where seemingly a zephyr gliding off the pads strikes it.

The fore part of this month was the warmest weather we have had; the last part, sloping toward the autumn, has reflected some of its coolness, for we are very forward to anticipate the fall. Perhaps I may say the spring culminated with the commencement of haying, and the summer side of the year in mid-July.

August

It is now the royal month of August.

A green bittern comes, noiselessly flapping, with stealthy and inquisitive looking to this side the stream and then that, thirty feet above the water. This antediluvian bird, creature of the night, is a fit emblem of a dead stream like this Musketicook. This especially is the bird of the river. There is a sympathy between its sluggish flight and the sluggish flow of the stream—its slowly lapsing flight, even like the rills of the Musketicook and my own pulse sometimes.

As I stand on the bank there [at Clamshell], I find suddenly that I hear, low and steady, under all other sounds, the creak of the mole cricket by the riverside. It has a peculiarly late sound, suggestive of the progress of the year. It is the voice which comes steadily at this season from that narrow sandy strip between the meadow and the water's edge. You might think it issued from that small frog, the only living thing you see, which sits so motionless on the sand. But the singer is wholly out of sight in his gallery under the surface. *Creak, creak, creak, creak, creak, creak, creak, creak.* It is a sound associated with the declining year and recalls the moods of that season. It is so unobtrusive yet universal a sound, so underlying the other sounds which fill the air—the song of birds, rustling of leaves, dry hopping sound of grasshoppers, etc.—that now, in my chamber,[1] I can hardly be sure whether I hear it still, or remember it, it so rings in my ears.

Just after bathing at the rock near the Island this afternoon, after sunset, I saw a flock of thousands of barn swallows and some white-bellied, and perhaps others, for it was too dark to distinguish them. They came flying over the river in loose array, wheeled and flew round in a great circle over the bay, there, about eighty feet high, with a loud twittering as if seeking a resting place, then flew up the stream. I was very much surprised at their numbers.

Directly after, hearing a buzzing sound, we found them all alighted on the dense golden willow hedge at Shattuck's shore, parallel with the shore, quite densely leaved and eighteen feet high. They were generally perched five or six feet from the top, amid the thick leaves, filling it for

---

[1] Here is revealed Thoreau's usual practice in the making of his *Journal*. On his walks he always carried pencil and paper for the recording of the instant impression. The next day, or perhaps days later, he expanded his "field notes" in his *Journal*. This ordinarily was the morning's task in his chamber. Then the afternoon was generally given over to his explorations of the Concord countryside, ashore and afloat.

eight or ten rods. They were very restless, fluttering from one perch to another and about one another, and kept up a loud and remarkable buzzing or squeaking, breathing or hum, with only occasionally a regular twitter, now and then flitting alongside from one end of the row to the other. It was so dark we had to draw close to see them.

At intervals they were perfectly still for a moment, as if at a signal. At length, after twenty or thirty minutes of bustle and hum, they all settled quietly to rest on their perches, I supposed for the night. We had rowed up within a rod of one end of the row, looking up so as to bring the birds between us and the sky, but they paid not the slightest attention to us. What was remarkable was: first, their numbers; second, their perching on densely leaved willows; third, their buzzing or humming, like a hive of bees, even squeaking notes; and fourth, their disregarding our nearness. I supposed that they were preparing to migrate, being the early broods.

Aug. 5. 4 P.M.—On river to see swallows.

They are all gone; yet Fay saw them there last night after we passed. Probably they started very early. I asked Minott if he ever saw swallows migrating, not telling him what I had seen, and he said that [he] used to get up and go out to mow very early in the morning on his meadow, as early as he could see to strike, and once, at that hour, hearing a noise, he looked up and could just distinguish high overhead fifty thousand swallows. He thought it was in the latter part of August.

As I wade through the middle of the meadows in sedge up to my middle and look afar over the waving and rustling bent tops of the sedge—all are bent northeast by the southwest wind—toward the distant mainland, I feel a little as if caught by a rising tide on flats far from the shore. I am,

as it were, cast away in the midst of the sea. It is a level
sea of waving and rustling sedge about me. The grassy sea.
You feel somewhat as you would if you were standing in
water at an equal distance from the shore. Today I can
walk dry over the greater part of the meadows, but not
over the lower parts, where pipes, etc., grow; yet many
think it has not been so dry for ten years! Goodwin is there
after snipes. I scare up one in the wettest part.

As we rest in our boat under a tree, we hear from time
to time the loud snap of a wood pewee's bill overhead,
which is incessantly diving to this side and that after an
insect and returning to its perch on a dead twig. We hear
the sound of its bill when it catches one.

Just opposite this bay [Lily Bay in the Sudbury Meadows]
I hear a peculiar note which I thought at first might be
that of a kingbird, but soon saw for the first time a wren
within two or three rods perched on the tall sedge or the
wool-grass and making it—probably the short-billed marsh
wren. It was peculiarly brisk and rasping, not at all musical, the rhythm something like *shar te dittle ittle ittle ittle
ittle,* but the last part was drier and less liquid than this
implies. It was a small bird, quite dark above and apparently plain ashy-white beneath, and held its head up when
it sang, and also commonly its tail. It dropped into the deep
sedge on our approach, but did not go off, as we saw by the
motion of the grass; then reappeared and uttered its brisk
notes quite near us, and flying off, was lost in the sedge
again. . . .
While bathing at Rice's landing, I noticed under my arm
amid the potamogeton, a little pickerel between two and
a half and three inches long, with a little silvery minnow
about one inch long in its mouth. He held it by the tail,
as it was jerking to and fro, and was slowly taking it in by

jerks. I watched to see if he turned it, but to my surprise he at length swallowed it tail foremost, the minnow struggling to the last and going alive into his maw. Perhaps the pickerel learn by experience to turn them head downward. Thus early do these minnows fall on fate, and the pickerel too fulfills his destiny.

More dog days. The sun, now at 9 A.M. has not yet burst through the mists. It has been warmer weather for a week than for at least three weeks before—nights when all windows were left open, though not so warm as in June. This morning a very heavy fog.

I find that we are now in the midst of the meadow-haying season, and almost every meadow or section of a meadow has its band of half a dozen mowers and rakers, either bending to their manly work with regular and graceful motion or resting in the shade, while the boys are turning the grass to the sun. I passed as many as sixty or a hundred men thus at work today. They stick up a twig with the leaves on, on the river's brink, as a guide for the mowers, that they may not exceed the owner's bounds. I hear their scythes cronching the coarse weeds by the river's brink as I row near. The horse or oxen stand near at hand in the shade on the firm land, waiting to draw home a load anon. I see a platoon of three or four mowers, one behind the other, diagonally advancing with regular sweeps across the broad meadow and ever and anon standing to whet their scythes. Or else, having made several bouts, they are resting in the shade on the edge of the firm land. In one place I see one sturdy mower stretched on the ground amid his oxen in the shade of an oak, trying to sleep; or I see one wending far inland with a jug to some well-known spring. . . .

Now Lee and his men are returning to their meadow-haying after dinner, and stop at the well under the black oak in the field. I too repair to the well when they are gone, and taste the flavor of blackstrap on the bucket's edge.[2] As I return down stream, I see the haymakers now raking with hand or horse rakes into long rows or loading, one on the load placing it and treading it down, while others fork it up to him; and others are gleaning with rakes after the forkers.

A great part of the farmers of Concord are now in the meadows and toward night great loads of hay are seen rolling slowly along the river's bank—on the firmer ground there—and perhaps fording the stream itself, toward the distant barn, followed by a troop of tired haymakers.

1.30 A.M.—Full moon. Arose and went to the river and bathed, stepping very carefully not to disturb the household, and still carefully in the street not to disturb the neighbors. . . .

Sitting on the sleepers of Hubbard's Bridge, which is being repaired, now, at 3 o'clock A.M.?, I hear a cock crow. How admirably adapted to the dawn is that sound! as if made by the first rays of light rending the darkness, the creaking of the sun's axle heard already over the eastern hills.

I walk over on the string pieces, resting in the middle until the moon comes out of a cloud, that I may see my path, for between the next piers the string-pieces also are removed, and there is only a rather narrow plank, let down three or four feet. I essay to cross it, but it springs a little

---

[2] Blackstrap—a judicious mixture of old Medford rum and molasses without which no ship was ever launched, no frame raised and no hay or ice made in the days of the West India trade. Contemporaneously described as "the sweetest drink that ever streaked down a gullet."

and I mistrust myself, whether I shall not plunge into the
river. Some demonic genius seems to be warning me. At-
tempt not the passage; you will surely be drowned. It is
very real that I am thus affected. Yet I am fully aware of
the absurdity of minding such suggestions. I put out my
foot, but I am checked, as if that power had laid a hand
on my breast and chilled me back. Nevertheless I cross,
stooping at first, and gain the other side. . . .

It is easy to see how, by yielding to such feelings as this,
men would re-establish all the superstitions of antiquity.
It is best that reason should govern us, and not those blind
intimations, in which we exalt our fears into a genius.

As I am paddling up the north side above the Hemlocks,
I am attracted by the singular shadows of the white lily
pads on the rich brown muddy bottom. It is remarkable
how light tends to prevail over shadow there. It steals in
under the densest curtain of pads and illustrates the bottom.

P.M.—to Barrett's Bar [by the Great Meadows] . . .

When I reached the upper end of this weedy bar, at
about 3 P.M., this warm day, I noticed some light colored
object in mid-river, near the other end of the bar. At first
I thought of some large stake or board standing amid the
weeds there, then of a fisherman in a brown holland sack,
referring him to the shore beyond. Supposing it the last,
I floated nearer and nearer till I saw plainly enough the
motions of the person whoever it was, and that it was no
stake. Looking through my glass thirty or forty rods off,
I thought certainly that I saw C., who had just bathed,
making signals to me with his towel, for I referred the
object to the shore twenty rods further. I saw his motions
as he wiped himself—the movements of his elbows and his
towel. Then I saw that the person was nearer and therefore smaller, that it stood on the sand-bar in midstream

in shallow water and must be some maiden [in] a bathing dress—for it was the color of brown holland web—and a very peculiar kind of dress it seemed.

But about this time I discovered with my naked eye that it was a blue heron standing in very shallow water amid the weeds of the bar and pluming itself. I had not noticed its legs at all, and its head, neck, and wings, being constantly moving, I had mistaken for arms, elbows and towel of a bather, and when it stood stiller its shapely body looked like a peculiar bathing-dress. I floated to within twenty-five rods and watched it at my leisure.

Standing on the shallowest part of the bar at that end, it was busily dressing its feathers, passing its bill like a comb down its feathers from base to tip. From its form and color, as well as size, it was singularly distinct. Its great spear-shaped head and bill was very conspicuous, though least so when turned toward me—whom it was eyeing from time to time. It coils its neck away upon its back or breast as a sailor might a rope, but occasionally stretches itself to its full height, as tall as a man, and looks around and at me. Growing shy, it begins to wade off, until its body is partly immersed amid the weeds—potamogetons—and then it looks more like a goose. The neck is continually varying in length, as it is doubled up or stretched out, and the legs also, as it wades in deeper or shallower water.

Suddenly comes a second, flying low, and alights on the bar yet nearer to me, almost high and dry. Then I hear a note from them, perhaps of warning—a short, coarse, frog-like purring or eructating sound. You might easily mistake it for a frog. I heard it half a dozen times. It was not very loud. Anything but musical. The last proceeds to plume himself, looking warily at me from time to time, while the other continues to edge off through the weeds. Now and then the latter holds its neck as if it were ready to strike its prey—stretched forward over the water—but I saw no

stroke. The arch may be lengthened or shortened, single
or double, but the great spear-shaped bill and head are
ever the same. A great hammer or pick, prepared to trans-
fix fish, frog, or bird.

At last the water becoming too deep for wading this one
takes easily to wing—though up to his body in water—and
flies a few rods to shore. It rather flies, then, than swims.
It was evidently scared. These were probably birds of this
season. I saw some distinct ferruginous on the angle of the
wing. There they stood in the midst of the open river, on
this shallow and weedy bar in the sun, the leisurely sentries,
lazily pluming themselves, as if the day were too long for
them. They gave a new character to the stream. Adjutant
they were to my idea of the river, these two winged men.

You have not seen our weedy river, you do not know the
significance of its weedy bars, until you have seen the blue
heron wading and pluming itself on it.

The hibiscus flowers are seen a quarter of a mile off over
the water, like large roses, now that these high colors are
rather rare. Some are exceedingly delicate and pale, almost
white, just rose-tinted, others a brighter pink or rose color,
and all slightly plaited—the five large petals—and turned
toward the sun, now in the west, trembling in the wind.
So much color looks very rich in these localities. The flowers
are some four inches in diameter, as large as water lilies,
rising amid and above the button bushes and willows, with
a large light green tree-like leaf and a stem half an inch
in diameter, apparently dying down to a perennial (?) root
each year.

A superb flower. Where it occurs, it is certainly, next to
the white lily, if not equally with it, the most spendid ornament of the river. Looking up the gleaming river, reflecting
the August sun, the round-topped silvery *white* maples,
the glossy-leaved swamp white oaks, the ethereal and buoy-

ant *Salix Purshiana*—the first and last resting on the water and giving the river a full appearance—and the hibiscus flowers adorning the shores, contrasting with the green across the river, close to the water's edge, the meadows being just shorn, all make a perfect August scene.

I name the shore under Fair Haven Hill the Cardinal Shore from the abundance of cardinal flowers there.[3]

The purple utricularia is *the* flower of the river today, apparently in its prime. It is very abundant, far more than any other utricularia, especially from Fair Haven Pond upward. That peculiar little bay in the pads, just below the inlet of the river, I will call Purple Utricularia Bay, from its prevalence there. I count a dozen within a square foot, one or two inches above the water, and they tinge the pads with purple for more than a dozen rods. I can distinguish their color thus far. The buds are the darkest or deepest purple.

Entered Fair Haven at sunset. . . .

As the rays of the sun fell horizontally across the placid pond, they lit up the side of Baker's Pleasant Meadow Wood which covers a hill. The different shades of green of different and the same trees—alders, pines, birch, maple, oak, etc.—melting into one another on their rounded bosky edges, made a most glorious soft and harmonious picture, only to be seen at this season of the day and perhaps of the year. It was a beautiful green rug with lighter shadings and rounded figures like the outlines of trees and shrubs of different shades of green. In the case of a single tree there

---

[3] Here is evidence of a quaint and interesting conceit. Thoreau was prone to give to particular localities his own names and his *Journal* abounds with them.—Conantum, Clematis and Nut Meadow Brooks, Andromeda and Cassandra Ponds, Bittern Cliff, Leaning Hemlocks, Owl Nest Swamp, Clamshell Hill—these are but a few of the colorful place names he invented.

was a dark glossy green of the lower, older leaves—the spring growth—which hang down, fading on every side into the silver hoariness of the younger and more downy leaves on the edges—the fall growth—whose under sides are seen, which stand up, and more perhaps at this hour. This was also the case with every bush along the river—the larger glossy dark-green watery leaves beneath and in the recesses, the upright hoary leaves whose under sides were seen on the shoots which rose above.

I never saw a forest-side look more luxuriantly and at the same time freshly beautiful. These lighter shades in the rug had the effect of watered silks—the edges lit, the breasts dark green, almost the cast on green crops seen by moonlight.

I have spliced my old sail to a new one, and now go out to try it in a sail to Baker Farm [on the east side of Fair Haven Bay]. It is a "square sail," some five feet by six. I like it much. It pulls like an ox, and makes me think there's more wind abroad than there is. The yard goes about with a pleasant force, almost enough, I would fain imagine, to knock me overboard. How sturdily it pulls, shooting us along, catching more wind than I knew to be wandering in this river valley! It suggests a new power in the sail, like a Grecian god. I can even worship it, after a heathen fashion. And then, how it becomes my boat and the river —a simple homely square sail, all for use not show, so low and broad! *Ajacean.* The boat is like a plow drawn by a winged bull. . . .

At Baker Farm a large bird rose up near us, which at first I took for a hen-hawk, but it appeared larger. It screamed the same, and finally soared higher and higher till it was almost lost amid the clouds, or could scarcely be distinguished except when it was seen against some white and glowing cumulus. I think it was at least half a mile high, or three quarters, and yet I distinctly heard it scream up there each time it came round, and with my glass saw its head steadily bent toward the ground, looking for its prey. Its head, seen in a proper light, was distinctly whitish, and I suspect it may have been a white-headed eagle. It did not once flap its wings up there, as it circled and sailed, though I watched it for nearly a mile. How fit that these soaring birds should be haughty and fierce, not like doves to our race!

The bright crimson-red under sides of the great white lily pads, turned up by the wind in broad fields on the sides of the stream, are a great ornament to the stream. . . . The surface being agitated the wind catches under their edges and turns them up and holds them commonly at an angle of 45°. It is a very wholesome color, and after the calm summer, an exhilarating sight, with a strong wind heard and felt, cooling and condensing your thoughts. This has the effect of a ripening of the leaf on the river. Not in vain was the under side thus colored, which at length the August winds turn up.

I hear part of a phoebe's strain, as I go over the railroad bridge. It is the voice of dying summer. . . .

Opened one of my snapping turtle's eggs. The egg was not warm to the touch. The young is now larger and darker colored, shell and all, more than a hemisphere, and the yolk which maintains it is much reduced. Its shell, very deep, hemispherical, fitting close to the shell of the egg, and, if you had not just opened the egg, you would say it could not contain so much. Its shell is considerably hardened, its feet and claws developed, and also its great head, though held in for want of room. Its eyes are open. It puts out its head, stretches forth its claws, and liberates its tail, though all were enveloped in a gelatinous fluid. With its great head it has already the ugliness of the full-grown, and is already a hieroglyphic of snappishness. It may take a fortnight longer to hatch it.

How much lies quietly buried in the ground that we wot not of! We unconsciously step over the eggs of snapping turtles slowly hatching the summer through. Not only was the surface perfectly dry and trackless there, but blackberry vines had run over the spot where these eggs were buried and weeds had sprung up above. If Iliads are not composed in our day, snapping turtles are hatched and arrive at maturity.

From the shore I hear only the creak of crickets. The winds of autumn begin to blow. Now I can sail. The cardinal flowers, almost drowned in a foot or two of water, are still very brilliant. The wind is Septemberish. That rush, reed, or sedge with the handsome head rises above the water. I pass boats now far from the shore and full of water. I see and hear the kingfisher with his disproportionate black [sic] head or crest. The pigeon woodpecker darts across the valley; a catbird mews in the alders; a great bittern flies sluggishly away from his pine tree perch on Tupelo Cliff, digging his way through the air. These and crows at long intervals are all the birds seen or heard. . . .

Landed at Lee's Cliff, in Fair Haven Pond, and sat on the Cliff. Late in the afternoon. The wind is gone down; the water is smooth; a serene evening is approaching; the clouds are dispersing; the sun has shone once or twice, but is now in a cloud. The pond, so smooth and full of reflections after a dark and breezy day, is unexpectedly beautiful.

There is a little boat on it, schooner rigged, with three sails, a perfect little vessel and perfectly reflected now in the water. It is sufficient life for the pond. Being in the reflection of the opposite woods, the water on which it rests—for there is hardly a puff of air, and the boatman is

only airing his sails after the storm—is absolutely invisible;
only the junction of the reflections shows where it must
be, and it makes an agreeable impression of buoyancy and
lightness as of a feather. The broad, dense, and now lower
and flatter border of button bushes, having water on both
sides, is very rich and moss-like, seen from this height, with
an irregular outline, being flooded while verdurous. The
sky is reflected on both sides, and no finer edging can
be imagined. A sail is, perhaps, the largest white object that
can be admitted into the landscape. It contrasts well with
the water, and is the most agreeable of regular forms. . . .

I float slowly down from Fair Haven till I have passed
the bridge. The sun, half an hour high, has come out again
just before setting, with a brilliant, warm light, and there
is the slightest undulation discernible on the water, from
the boat or other cause, as it were its imitation in glass. The
reflections are perfect. A bright fresh green on fields and
trees now after the rain, spring-like with the sense of summer past. The reflections are more perfect for the blackness
of the water. I see the down of a thistle, probably, in the
air descending to the water two or three rods off, which I
mistake for a man in his shirtsleeves descending a distant
hill, by an ocular delusion. How fair the smooth green swells
of those low grassy hills on which the sunlight falls! Indian
hills.

This is the most glorious part of this day, the serenest,
warmest, brightest part, and the most suggestive. Evening
is fairer than morning. It is chaste eve, for it has sustained
the trials of the day but to the morning such praise was in-
applicable. It is incense-breathing. Morning is full of promise and vigor. Evening is pensive. The serenity is far more
remarkable to those who are on the water.

That part of the sky just above the horizon seen reflected,
apparently some rods off from the boat, is as light a blue
as the actual, but it goes on deepening as your eye draws

nearer to the boat, until, when you look directly down at the reflection of the zenith, it is lost in the blackness of the water. It passes through all degrees of dark blue, and the threatening aspect of a cloud is very much enhanced in the reflection. As I wish to be on the water at sunset, I let the boat float. . . .

A flock of half a dozen or more blue-winged teal, scared up down stream behind me, as I was rowing, have circled round to reconnoitre and cross up stream before me, quite close. I had seen another flock of ducks high in the air in the course of the day. Have ducks then begun to return?

On the 31st of August 1839, there commenced the famous excursion of the brothers Thoreau that is recounted in A Week on the Concord and Merrimack Rivers. *The following passages derive from this source.*

At length, on Saturday, the last day of August, 1839, we two, brothers, and natives of Concord, weighed anchor in this river port; for Concord, too, lies under the sun, a port of entry and departure for the bodies as well as the souls of men; one shore at least exempted from all duties but such as an honest man will gladly discharge. A warm, drizzling rain had obscured the morning, and threatened to delay our voyage, but at length the leaves and grass were dried, and it came out a mild afternoon, as serene and fresh as if Nature were maturing some great scheme of her own. After this long dripping and oozing from every pore, she began to respire again more healthily than ever. So with a vigorous shove we launched our boat from the bank, while the flags and bulrushes courtesied a God-speed, and dropped silently down the stream. . . .

Gradually the village murmer subsided, and we seemed to be embarked on the placid current of our dreams, floating from past to future as silently as one awakes to fresh morning or evening thoughts. We glided noiselessly down the stream, occasionally driving a pickerel or a bream from the covert of the pads, and the smaller bittern now and then sailed away on sluggish wings from some recess in the shore, or the larger lifted itself out of the long grass at our approach, and carried its precious legs away to deposit them in a place of safety. The tortoises also rapidly dropped into the water, as our boat ruffled the surface amid the willows, breaking the reflections of the trees. The banks had passed the height of their beauty, and some of the brighter flowers showed by their faded tints that the season was verging towards the afternoon of the year; but this sombre tinge enhanced their sincerity, and in the still unabated heats they seemed like the mossy brink of some cool well.

The narrow-leaved willow (*Salix Purshiana*) lay along the surface of the water in masses of light green foliage, interspersed with the large balls of the button bush. The small rose-colored polygonum raised its head proudly above the water on either hand, and flowering at this season and in these localities, in front of dense fields of the white species which skirted the sides of the stream, its little streak of red looked very rare and precious. The pure white blossoms of the arrow-head stood in the shallower parts, and a few cardinals on the margin still proudly surveyed themselves reflected in the water, though the latter, as well as the pickerel weed, was now nearly out of blossom. The snake-head (*Chelone glabra*) grew close to the shore, while a kind of coreopsis, turning its brazen face to the sun, full and rank, and a tall, dull red flower (*Eupatorium purpureum*, or trumpet-weed) formed the rear rank of the fluvial array. The bright blue flowers of the soapwort gentian were sprinkled here and there in the adjacent meadows, like flowers which Proserpine had dropped, and still farther in the fields or higher on the bank were seen the purple Gerardia, the Virginian rhexia, and drooping neottia or ladies-tresses; while from the more distant waysides which we occasionally passed, and banks where the sun had lodged, was reflected still a dull yellow beam from the ranks of tansy, now past its prime.

In short, Nature seemed to have adorned herself for our departure with a profusion of fringes and curls, mingled with the bright tints of flowers, reflected in the water. . . .

From this point [Ball's Hill] the river runs perfectly straight for a mile or more to Carlisle Bridge, which consists of twenty wooded piers, and when we looked back over it, its surface was reduced to a line's breadth and appeared like a cobweb gleaming in the sun. Here and there might be seen a pole sticking up, to mark the place where some fisherman had enjoyed unusual luck, and in return had consecrated his rod to the deities who preside over these shallows. It was full twice as broad as before, deep and tranquil, with a muddy bottom, and bordered with willows, beyond which spread broad lagoons covered with pads, bulrushes, and flags.

Late in the afternoon we passed a man on the shore fishing with a long birch pole, its silvery bark left on, and a dog at his side, rowing so near as to agitate his cork with our oars, and drive away luck for a season; and when we had rowed a mile as straight as an arrow, with our faces turned towards him, and the bubbles in our wake still visible on the tranquil surface, there stood the fisher still with his dog, like statues under the other side of the heavens, the only objects to relieve the eye in the extended meadow; and there would he stand abiding his luck, till he took his way home through the fields at evening with his fish. Thus, by one bait or another, Nature allures inhabitants into all her recesses. This man was the last of our townsmen whom we saw, and we silently through him bade adieu to our friends.

September

From Ball's Hill to Billerica meeting-house the river is a noble stream of water, flowing between gentle hills and occasional cliffs, and well wooded all the way. It can hardly be said to flow at all, but rests in the lap of the hills like a quiet lake. The boatmen call it a dead stream. For many long reaches you can see nothing to indicate that men inhabit its banks. Nature seems to hold a sabbath herself today—a still warm sun on the river and wood, and not breeze enough to ruffle the water. Cattle stand up to their bellies in the river, and you think Rembrandt should be here.

119

The river nowadays is a permanent mirror stretching without end through the meadows, and unfailingly when I look out my window across the dusty road, I see it at a distance with the herbage of its brink reflected in it. There it lies, a mirror uncracked, unsoiled.

The river smooth, though full, with the autumn sheen on it, as on the leaves. I see painted tortoises with their entire backs covered with perfectly fresh clean black scales, such as no rubbing nor varnishing can produce contrasting advantageously with brown and muddy ones. One little one floats past on a drifting pad which he partly sinks.

Paddled to Baker Farm just after sundown, by full moon. . . .

It was in harmony with this fair evening that we were not walking or riding with dust and noise through it, but moved by a paddle without a jar over the liquid and almost invisible surface, floating directly toward those islands of the blessed which we call clouds in the sunset sky. I thought of the Indian, who so many similar evenings had paddled up this stream, with what advantage he beheld the twilight sky. So we advanced without dust or sound, by gentle influences, as the twilight gradually faded away. The height of the railroad bridge, already high—more than twenty feet to the top of the rail—was doubled by the reflection, equalling that of a Roman aqueduct, for we could not possibly see where the reflection began, and the piers appeared to rise from the lowest part of the reflection to the rail above, about fifty feet. We floated directly under it, between the piers, as if in mid-air, not being able to distinguish the surface of the water, and looked down more than twenty feet to the reflected flooring through whose intervals we saw the starlit sky. The ghostly piers stretched downward on all sides, and only the angle made by their meeting the real ones betrayed where was the water surface.

The twilight had now paled—lost its red and dun—and
faintly illumined the high bank. I observed no firefly this
evening, nor the 4th [three days previous]. The moon had
not yet risen and there was a half hour of dusk in which,
however, we saw the reflections of the trees. Any peculiarity
in the form of a tree or other object—if it leans one side
or has a pointed top, for instance—is revealed in the reflection by being doubled and so insisted on. We detected thus
distant maples, pines and oaks, and they were seen to be
related to the river as mountains in the horizon are by day.

Night is the time to hear; our ears took in every sound
from the meadows and the village. At first we were disturbed by the screeching of the locomotive and rumbling
of the cars, but soon were left to the fainter natural sounds
—the creaking of crickets, and the little *Rana palustris*[1]—I
am not sure that I heard it the latter part of the evening—
and the shrilling of other crickets (?), the occasional faint
lowing of a cow and the distant barking of dogs, as in a
whisper. Our ears drank in every sound. I heard once or
twice a dumping frog.

This was while we lay off Nut Meadow Brook waiting for
the moon to rise. She burned her way slowly through the
small but thick clouds, and, as fast as she triumphed over
them and rose over them, they appeared pale and shrunken,
like the ghosts of their former selves. Meanwhile we measured the breadth of the clear cope over our heads, which
she would ere long traverse, and, while she was concealed,
looked up to the few faint stars in the zenith which is ever
lighted. C. thought that these few faint lights in the ever-
lit sky, whose inconceivable distance was enhanced by a
few downy wisps of cloud, surpassed any scene that earth
could show. When the moon was behind those small black
clouds in the horizon, they had a splendid silver edging.

---

[1] ["Mole cricket" is here substituted in pencil for "*Rana palustris*."]

At length she rose above them and shone aslant, like a ball of fire over the woods.

It was remarkably clear tonight, and the water was not so remarkably broad therefore, and Fair Haven was not clothed with that blue veil like a mountain, which it wore on the 4th, but it was not until we had passed the bridge that the first sheen was reflected from the pads. The reflected shadow of the Hill was black as night, and we seemed to be paddling directly into it a rod or two before us, but we never reached it at all. The trees and hills were distinctly black between us and the moon, and the water black or gleaming accordingly. It was quite dry and warm.

Above the Cliffs we heard only one or two owls at a distance, a hooting owl and a screech owl and several whip-poor-wills. The delicious fragrance of ripe grapes was wafted to us by the night air, as we paddled by, from every fertile vine on the shore, and thus its locality was revealed more surely than by daylight. We knew their fragrance better than their flavor. They perfumed the whole river for a mile, by night. You might have thought you had reached the confines of Elysium.

A slight zephyr wafted us almost imperceptibly into the middle of Fair Haven Pond, while we lay watching and listening. The sheen of the moon extended quite across the pond to us in a long and narrow triangle, or rather with concave sides like a very narrow Eddystone Lighthouse, with its base on the southwest shore, and we heard the distant sound of the wind through the pines on the hilltop. Or, if we listened closely, we heard still the faint and distant barking of dogs. They rule the night. Near the south shore disturbed some ducks in the water, which slowly flew away to seek a new resting place, uttering a distinct and alarmed *quack* something like a goose. . . .

Returning later, we experienced better the weird-like character of the night, especially perceived the fragrance of the grapes and admired the fair smooth fields in the bright moonlight. There being no mist, the reflections were wonderfully distinct; the whole of Bittern Cliff with its grove was seen beneath the waves.

They left the boat that night in the lee of Fair Haven Hill and Thoreau returned to it the next afternoon to go "a-graping."

The grapes would no doubt be riper a week hence, but I am compelled to go now before the vines are stripped. I partly smell them out. I pluck splendid great bunches of the purple ones, with a rich bloom on them and the purple glowing through it like a fire; large red ones, also, with light dots, and some clear green. Sometimes I crawl under low and thick bowers where they have run over the alders only four or five feet high, and see the grapes hanging from a hollow hemisphere of leaves over my head. At other times I see them dark-purple or black against the silvery undersides of the leaves, high overhead where they have run over birches or maples, and either climb or pull them down to pluck them. . . .

I have brought home a half-bushel of grapes to scent my chamber with. It is impossible to get them home in a basket with all their rich bloom on them, which, no less than the form of the clusters, makes their beauty. As I paddled home with my basket of grapes in the bow, every now and then their perfume was wafted to me in the stern, and I thought I was passing a richly laden vine on shore. Some goldfinches twitter over, while I am pulling down the vines from the birch tops. The ripest rattle off and strew the ground before I reach the clusters, or, while I am standing on tiptoe and endeavoring gently to break the tough peduncle, the petiole of a leaf gets entangled in the bunch and I am compelled to strip them all off loosely.

This hot September afternoon all may be quiet amid the weeds, but the dipper, and the bittern, and the yellowlegs and the blue heron, and the rail are silently feeding there. At length the walker who sits meditating on a distant bank sees the little dipper sail out from amid the weeds and busily dive for its food along their edge. Yet ordinary eyes might range up and down the river all day and never detect its small black head above the water.[2]

To Conantum *via* fields, Hubbard's Grove, and grain-field, to Tupelo Cliff and Conantum and returning over peak same way. 6 P.M. . . .

At Tupelo Cliff I hear the sound of singers on the river, young men and women—which is unusual here—returning from their row. Man's voice, thus uttered, fits well the spaces. It fills nature. And, after all, the singing of men is something far grander than any natural sound. It is wonderful that men do not oftener sing in the fields, by day and night. I bathe at the north side of the Cliff, while the moon shines round the end of the rock. The opposite Cliff is reflected in the water. Then sit on the south side of the Cliff in the woods. One or two fireflies. Could it be a glow-worm? I thought I saw one or two in the air. That is all in this walk. I hear a whip-poor-will uttering a cluck of suspicion in my rear. He is suspicious and inquisitive.

The river stretches off southward from me. I see the sheeny portions of its western shore interruptedly for a quarter of a mile, where the moonlight is reflected from the pads, a strong, gleaming light while the water is lost

---

[2] It was the view of the late Francis H. Allen that this dipper was a pied bill grebe, *Podilymbus podiceps podiceps*. One of the editors of Thoreau's *Journal* and an expert ornithologist, Mr. Allen's arrangement of the entries in the *Journal* relating to birds in his *Notes on New England Birds*, Boston, 1910, is the authoritative commentary upon all of Thoreau's ornithological observations.

in the obscurity. I hear the sound from time to time of a leaping fish, or a frog, or a muskrat, or turtle. It is even warmer, *methinks,* than it was in August and it is perfectly clear—the air. I know not how it is that this universal crickets' creak should sound thus regularly intermittent, as if for the most part they fell in with one another and creaked in time, making a certain pulsing sound, a sort of breathing or panting of all nature. You sit twenty feet above the still river; see the sheeny pads, and the moon, and some bare tree-tops in the distant horizon. Those bare tree-tops add greatly to the wildness.

Lower down I see the moon in the water as bright as in the heavens; only the water-bugs disturb its disk; and now I catch a faint glassy glare from the whole river surface, which before was simply dark. This is set in a frame of double darkness on the east, *i.e.,* the reflected shore of woods and hills and the reality, the shadow and the substance, bipartite, answering to each.

I see the northern lights over my shoulder, to remind me of the Esquimaux and that they are still my contemporaries on this globe, that they too are taking their walks on another part of the planet, in pursuit of seals, perchance. The stars are dimly reflected in the water. The path of water-bugs in the moon's rays is like ripples of light. It is only when you stand fronting the sun or moon that you see their light reflected in the water. I hear no frogs these nights—bullfrogs or others—as in the spring. It is not the season of sound.

At Conantum end, just under the wall. From this point and at this height I do not perceive any bright or yellowish light on Fair Haven, but an oily and glass-like smoothness on its southwestern bay, through a very slight mistiness. Two or three pines appear to stand in the moonlit air on this side of the pond, while the enlightened portion of the water is bounded by the heavy reflection of the wood on the east. It was so soft and velvety a light as contained a thousand placid days sweetly put to rest in the bosom of the water. So looked the North Twin Lake in the Maine woods.

The *Aster tradescanti,* now in its prime, sugars the banks all along the riverside with a profusion of small white blossoms resounding with the hum of bees. It covered the ground to the depth of two feet over large tracts, looking at a little distance somewhat like a smart hoar frost or sleet or sugaring on the weeds. The banks are sugared with the *A. tradescanti.*

Now, instead of haying, they are raking cranberries all along the river. The raker moves slowly along with a basket before him, into which he rakes (hauling) the berries, and his wagon stands one side. It is now the middle of the cranberry season.

Sept. 16. When I awake I hear the sound of steady heavy rain. A southeast storm. . . .

It rained as hard as I remember to have seen it for about five minutes at six o'clock P.M. when I was out, and then suddenly, as it were in an instant, the wind whirled round to the westward, and clear sky appeared there and the storm ended—which had lasted all day and part of the previous night.[3]

---

[3] This is a dramatic instance of the change in the weather along the New England coast that has given rise to the Down-easter's rule of thumb in forecasting. The east wind is the talisman. The prevailing winds are westerly and with them the weather is generally fair and stable. An easterly, however, or a southerly, brings unsettled weather, and if the wind hangs in that quarter or, as the phrase runs, tries to back around into the north, this means continuing bad weather. Only when she—in the vernacular— hauls round into the west, as it did so suddenly in the instance described by Thoreau, is there assurance of clear skies and fair weather.

A September storm such as this one is known in those parts as the "equinoctial" and it ushers in a spell of gorgeous blue and gold weather.

It is a fine September day. The river is still rising on ac-count of the rain of the 16th and is getting pretty well over the meadows. As we paddle westward toward College Meadow, I perceive that a new season has come. The air is incredibly clear. The surface of both land and water is bright, as if washed by the recent rain and then seen through a much finer, clearer, and cooler air. The surface of the river sparkles. I am struck by the soft yellow-brown or brown-yellow of the black willows, stretching in cloud-shaped wreaths far away along the edges of the stream of a so much mellower and maturer tint than the elms and oaks and most other trees seen above and beyond them. It is remarkable that the button bushes beneath and mingling with them are of exactly the same tint and in perfect harmony with them. They are like two interrupted long brown-yellow masses of verdure resting on the water, a peculiarly soft and warm yellow. This is, perhaps, the most interesting autumnal tint as yet. . . .

At Clamshell we take the wind again, and away we glide. I notice, along the edge of the eastern meadow wood, some very light-colored and crisped-looking leaves, apparently on small maples, or else swamp white oaks, as if some vine ran over the trees for the leaves are of a different color from the rest. This must be the effect of frost, I think.

I see ducks or teal flying silent, swift, and straight, the wild creatures.

Sept. 20. Melvin says that there are many teal about the river now.

Rain in the afternoon. Rain again in the night, hard.

Autumn

These are the stages in the river fall: first, the two varieties of yellow lily pads begin to decay and blacken (long ago); second, the first fall rains come after dog days and raise and cool the river, and winds wash the decaying sparganium, etc., to the shores and clear the channel more or less; third, when the first harder frosts come (as this year [1854] the 21st and 22d inst.), the button-bushes, which before had attained only a dull mixed yellow, are suddenly bitten, wither, and turn brown all but the protected parts.

The *first* fall is so gradual as not to make much impression, but the last suddenly and conspicuously gives a fall aspect to the scenery of the river. The button-bushes thus withered, covered still with the gray, already withered mikania, suddenly paint with a rich brown the river's brim. It is like the crust, the edging of a boy's turnover done brown. And the black willows, slightly faded and crisped with age or heat, enhance my sense of the year's maturity.

There, where the land appears to lap over the water by a mere edging, these thinner portions are first done brown. I float over the still liquid middle.

I have not seen any such conspicuous effect of frost as this sudden withering of the button-bushes. The muskrats make haste now to rear their cabins and conceal themselves.

What can be handsomer for a picture than our river scenery now?

Take this view from the first Conantum Cliff.[1] First this smoothly shorn meadow on the west side of the stream with all the swaths distinct, sprinkled with apple trees casting heavy shadows black as ink, such as can be seen only in this clear air, this strong light, one cow wandering restlessly about in it and lowing; then the blue river, scarcely darker than and not to be distinguished from the sky, its waves driven southward, or up-stream, by the wind, making it appear to flow that way bordered by willows and button-bushes; then the narrow meadow beyond with varied lights and shades from its waving grass, which for some reason has not been cut this year, though so dry, now at length each grass blade bending south before the wintry blast, as if bending for aid in that direction; then the hill rising sixty feet to a terrace-like plain covered with shrub oaks, maples, etc., now variously tinted, clad all in a livery of gay colors, every bush a feather in its cap; and further in the rear the wood-crowned Cliff some two hundred feet high, where gray rocks here and there project from amidst the bushes, with its orchard on the slope; and to the right of the Cliff the distant Lincoln Hills in the horizon.

---

[1] This interesting place-name derives from the fact that this ridge of land rising from the west shore of the Sudbury and facing Fair Haven Hill and Bay, was the property of a Conant. Thoreau merely tagged on the Latin suffix and this place-name of his has stuck to this day, now denoting a modern housing development on the site.

The landscape so handsomely colored, the air so clear and wholesome; and the surface of the earth is so pleasingly varied, that it seems rarely fitted for the abode of man.

The collection from the shores of the river of wood for his fire in his chamber during the winter was a customary stint in each fall of the year.

Brought home quite a boat-load of fuel—one oak rail, on which fishers had stood in wet ground at Bittern Cliff, a white pine rider (?) with a square hole in [it] made by a woodpecker anciently, so wasted the sap as to leave the knots projecting, several chestnut rails; and I obtained behind Cardinal Shore a large oak stump which I know to have been bleaching there for more than thirty years, with three great gray prongs sprinkled with lichens. It bore above the marks of the original burning. There was a handful of hazel-nuts under it emptied by the ground (?) squirrel, a pretty large hole in the rough and thin stem end of each, where the bur was attached. Also, at Clamshell Hill Shore, a chestnut boat-post, with a staple in it, which the ice took up last winter, though it had an arm put through it two feet underground. Some much decayed perhaps old red maple stumps at Hubbard's Bath Place.

It would be a triumph to get all my winter's wood thus. How much better than to buy a cord coarsely from a farmer, seeing that I get my money's worth! Then it only affords me a momentary satisfaction to see the pile tipped up in the yard. Now I derive a separate and peculiar pleasure from every stick that I find. Each has its history, of which I am reminded when I come to burn it, and under what circumstances I found it. Got home late C. [Channing] and I supped together after our work at wooding, and talked it over with great appetites.

A.M. Sawing up my raft by river.

River about thirty-five inches above summer level and goes no higher this time.

Monroe's tame ducks sail along and feed close to me as I am working there. Looking up I see a little dipper, about one half their size, in the middle of the river, evidently attracted by these tame ducks, as to a place of security. I sit down and watch it.

The tame ducks have paddled four or five rods down stream along the shore. They soon detect the dipper three or four rods off, and betray alarm by a tittering note, especially when it dives, as it does continually. At last when it is two or three rods off and approaching them by diving, they all rush to the shore and come out on it in their fear, but the dipper shows itself close to the shore, and when they enter the water again joins them within two feet, still diving from time to time and threatening to come up in their midst. They return upstream, more or less alarmed, and pursued in this wise by the dipper, who does not know what to make of their fears, and soon the dipper is thus tolled along to within twenty feet of where I sit, and I can watch it at my leisure.

It has a dark bill and considerable white on the sides of the head or neck, with black between it, no tufts, and no observable white on back or tail. When at last disturbed by me, it suddenly sinks low (all its body) in the water without diving.

A.M.—Up the Assabet.

The river is considerably raised and also muddied by the recent rains.

I saw a red squirrel run along the bank under the hemlocks with a nut in its mouth. He stopped near the foot of a hemlock, and, hastily pawing a hole with his forefeet, dropped the nut, covered it up, and retreated part way up the trunk of the tree, all in a few moments. I approached the shore to examine the deposit, and he, descending betrayed no little anxiety for his treasure and made two or three motions to recover the nut before he retreated. Digging there, I found two pignuts joined together, with their green shells on, buried about an inch and a half in the soil, under the red hemlock leaves.

This then is the way forests are planted. This nut must have been brought twenty rods at least and was buried at just the right depth. If the squirrel is killed, or neglects its deposit, a hickory springs up.

A very fine and warm afternoon after a cloudy morning. Carry Aunt and Sophia a-barberrying to Conantum. . . .

We got about three pecks of barberries[2] from four or five bushes, but I filled my fingers with prickles to pay for them. With the hands well defended, it would be pleasant picking, they are so handsome and beside are so abundant and fill up so fast. I take hold of the end of the drooping twigs with my left hand, raise them, and then strip downward at once as many clusters as my hand will embrace, commonly bringing away with the raceme two small green leaves or bracts, which I do not stop to pick out. When I come to a particularly thick and handsome wreath of fruit, I pluck the twig entire and bend it around the inside of the basket. Some bushes bear much larger and plumper berries than others. Some also are comparatively green yet.

Meanwhile the catbird mews in the alders by my side, and the scream of the jay is heard from the woodside. When

---

[2] The red berries, *Berberis canadensis,* were used to make a preserve and often added to other preserved fruits to impart a tart flavor. In former days the barberry was in use, according to Culpeper's Complete Herbal, as a "remedy to cleanse the body of choleric humours" . . . being "excellent for hot agues, burnings, scaldings, heat of the blood, heat of the liver, bloody flux, for the berries are as good as the bark, and more pleasing; they get a man a good stomach to his victuals. . . ."

returning about 4.30 P.M. we observed a slight mistiness, a sea-turn advancing from the east, and soon after felt the raw east wind—quite a contrast to the air we had before— and presently all the western woods are partially veiled with the mist. Aunt thought she could smell the salt marsh in it.

These are warm, serene, bright autumn afternoons. I see far off the various-colored gowns of cranberry-pickers against the green of the meadow. The river stands a little way over the grass again, and the summer is over.

P.M.—To Clamshell by boat.
  . . . Bathed at Hubbard's Bath, but found the water very cold. Bathing about over.
  It is a very fine afternoon to be on the water, somewhat Indian-summer-like. I do not know what constitutes the peculiarity and charm of this weather; the broad water so smooth, notwithstanding the slight wind, as if, owing to some oiliness, the wind slid over without ruffling it. There is a slight coolness in the air, yet the sun is occasionally very warm. I am tempted to say that the air is singularly clear, yet I see it is quite hazy. Perhaps it is that transparency it is said to possess when full of moisture and before or after rain. Through this I see colors of trees and shrubs beginning to put on their October dress, and the creak of the mole cricket sounds late along the shore.

Some single red maples now fairly make a show along the meadow. I see a blaze of red reflected from the troubled water.

The red maple has fairly begun to blush in some places by the river. I see one by the canal behind Barrett's mill, all aglow against the sun. These first trees that change are most interesting since they are seen against others still freshly green—such brilliant red on green. I go half a mile out of my way to examine such a red banner. A single tree becomes the crowning beauty of some meadowy vale and attracts the attention of the traveler from afar. At the eleventh hour of the year, some tree which has stood mute and inglorious in some distant vale thus proclaims its character as effectually as [if] it stood by the highway-side and it leads our thoughts away from the dusty road into those brave solitudes which it inhabits. The whole tree thus ripening in advance of its fellows, attains a singular preeminence. I am thrilled at the sight of it, bearing aloft its scarlet standard for its regiment of green-clad foresters around. The forest is the more spirited.

By boat to Fair Haven Pond. . . .

Red maples now fairly glow along the shore. They vary from yellow to a peculiar crimson which is more red than common crimson. But these particular trees soon fade. It is the first blush which is the purest. See men raking cranberries now, or far away squatting in the meadows where they are picking them. Grapes have begun to shrivel on their stems. They drop off on the slightest touch, and if they fall into the water are lost, going to the bottom. You see the grape leaves touched with frost curled up and looking crisp on their edges.

I am surprised to see that *some* red maples, which were so brilliant a day or two ago, have already shed their leaves, and they cover the land and water quite thickly. I see a countless fleet of them slowly carried round in the still bay by the Leaning Hemlocks.

A large flock of grackles amid the willows by the riverside, or chiefly concealed low in the button bushes beneath them, though quite near me. There they keep up their spluttering notes, though somewhat less loud methinks, than in spring. These are the first I have seen, and now for some time, I think, the redwings have been gone. These are the first arrivers from the north where they breed.

October

October—the month of ripe or painted leaves.

There is a great difference between this season and a month ago—warm as this happens to be—as between one period of your life and another. A little frost is at the bottom of it.

Some particular maple among a hundred will be of a peculiarly bright and pure scarlet, and, by its difference of

tint and intenser color, attract our eyes even at a distance
in the midst of the crowd. Looking all around Fair Haven
Pond yesterday, where the maples were glowing amid the
evergreens, my eyes invariably rested on a particular small
maple of the purest and intensest scarlet.

You cannot judge a tree by seeing it from one side only.
As you go round or away from it, it may overcome you with
its mass of glowing scarlet or yellow light. You need to
stand where the greatest number of leaves will transmit or
reflect to you most favorably. The tree which looked comparatively lifeless, cold, and merely parti-colored, seen in
a more favorable light as you are floating away from it,
may affect you wonderfully as a warm glowing drapery.
I now see one small red maple which is all a pure yellow
within and a bright red scarlet on its outer surface and
prominences. It is a remarkably distinct painting of scarlet
on a yellow ground. It is an indescribably beautiful contrast of scarlet and yellow. Another is yellow and green,
where this was scarlet and yellow, and in this case the
bright and liquid green, now getting to be rare, is by contrast as charming a color as the scarlet.

I met in the street afterward a young lady who rowed
up the river with me, and I could tell exactly where she
plucked the maple twig which she held in her hand. It was
the one so conspicuous for a quarter of a mile in one reach
of the river.

When I turn round half way up Fair Haven Hill by the
orchard wall and look northwest, I am surprised for the
thousandth time at the beauty of the landscape, and I sit
down to behold it at my leisure. I think that Concord affords no better view. It is always incredibly fair, but ordinarily we are mere objects in it, and not witnesses of it.
I see through the bright October air, a valley extending

southwest and northeast and some two miles across—so far I can see distinctly—with a broad, yellow meadow tinged with brown at the bottom, and a blue river winding slowly through it northward, with a regular edging of low bushes on the brink, of the same color with the meadow. Skirting the meadow are straggling lines, and occasionally large masses a quarter of a mile wide, of brilliant scarlet and yellow and crimson trees, backed by and mingled with green forests and green and hoary russet fields and hills; and on the hills around shoot up a million scarlet and orange and crimson fires amid the green; and here and there amid the trees, often beneath the largest and most graceful of those which have brown-yellow dome-like tops, are bright white or gray houses; and beyond stretches a forest, wreath upon wreath, and between each two wreaths I know lies a similar vale; and far beyond all, on the verge of the horizon, are half a dozen dark blue mountain summits.

7.30 P.M.—To Fair Haven Pond by boat, the moon four fifths full, not a cloud in the sky; paddling all the way. The water perfectly still, and the air almost, the former gleaming like oil in the moonlight, with the moon's disk reflected in it.

When we started, saw some fishermen kindling their fire for spearing by the riverside. It was a lurid, reddish blaze, contrasting with the white light of the moon, with dense volumes of black smoke from the burning pitch pine roots rolling upward in the form of an inverted pyramid. The blaze reflected in the water, almost as distinct as the substance. It looked like tarring a ship on the shore of the Styx or Cocytus. For it is still and dark, notwithstanding the moon, and no sound but the crackling of the fire. The fishermen can be seen only near at hand, though their fire is visible far away; and then they appear as dusky, fuliginous figures, half enveloped in smoke, seen only by their enlightened sides. Like devils they look, clad in old coats to defend

themselves from the fogs, one standing up forward holding the spear ready to dart, while the smoke and flames are
blown in his face, the other paddling the boat slowly and
silently along close to the shore with almost imperceptible
motion.

The river appears indefinitely wide; there is a mist rising
from the water, which increases the indefiniteness. . . .

Now the fisherman's fire, left behind, acquires some thick
rays in the distance and becomes a star. As surely as sunlight falling through an irregular chink makes a round figure on the opposite wall, so the blaze at a distance appears
a star. Such is the effect of the atmosphere. The bright sheen
of the moon is constantly traveling with us, and is seen
at the same angle in front on the surface of the pads; and
the reflection of its disk in the rippled water by our boat-
side appears like bright gold pieces falling on the river's
counter. This coin is incessantly poured forth as from some
unseen horn of plenty at our side. . . .

I shout like a farmer to his oxen—a short barking shout—
and instantly the woods on the eastern shore take it up,
and the western hills a little up the stream; and so it appears
to rebound from one side the river valley to the other, till
at length I hear a farmer call to his team far up as Fair
Haven Bay, whither we are bound. . . .

In the middle of the pond we tried the echo again.
First the hill to the right took it up; then further up the
stream on the left; and then after a long pause when we had
almost given it up—and the longer expected, the more in
one sense unexpected and surprising it was—we heard a
farmer shout to his team in a distant valley, far up on
the opposite side of the stream, much louder than the
previous echo; and even after this we heard one shout
faintly in some neighboring town. The third echo seemed
more loud and distinct than the second. But why, I asked,
do the echoes always travel up the stream? I turned about

and shouted again, and then I found that they all appeared equally to travel down the stream, or perchance I heard only those that did so. . . .

As we paddled down the stream with our backs to the moon, we saw the reflection of every wood and hill on both sides distinctly. These answering reflections—shadow to substance—impress the voyager with a sense of harmony and symmetry, as when you hold a blotted paper and produce a regular figure—a dualism which nature loves. What you commonly see is but half. Where the shore is very low the actual and reflected trees appear to stand foot to foot, and it is but a line that separates them, and the water and the sky almost flow into one another, and the shore seems to float. As we paddle up or down, we see the cabins of muskrats faintly rising from amid the weeds, and the strong odor of musk is borne to us from particular parts of the shore. Also the odor of a skunk is wafted from over the meadows or fields. The fog appears in some places gathered into a little pyramid or squad by itself on the surface of the water.

Home at ten.

The reach of the river between Bedford and Carlisle seen from a distance in the road to-day, as formerly, has a singularly ethereal, celestial, or elysian look. It is of a light sky-blue, alternating with smoother white streaks, where the surface reflects the light differently, like a milk-pan full of the milk of Valhalla partially skimmed, more gloriously and heavenly fair and pure than the sky itself. It is something more celestial than the sky above it. I never saw any water look so celestial. I have often noticed it. I believe I have seen this reach from the hill in the middle of Lincoln.

A very still, warm, bright, clear afternoon. Our boat so small and low that we are close to the water. The muskrats all the way [to Corner Bridge] are now building their houses, about two thirds done. . . . Seen at this stage they show some art and a good deal of labor. We pulled one to pieces to examine the inside. There was a small cavity, which might hold two or three full-grown muskrats, just above the level of the water, quite wet and of course dark and narrow, communicating immediately with a gallery under water. There were a few pieces of the white root of some water-plant—perhaps a pontederia or a lily root—in it.

There they dwell, in close contiguity to the water itself, always in a wet compartment, in a wet coat never changed, with immeasurable water in the cellar, through which is the only exit. They have reduced life to a lower scale than Diogenes.

Another perfect Indian summer day. One of my oars makes a creaking sound like a block in a harbor, such a sound as would bring tears into an old sailor's eyes. It suggests to me adventure and seeking one's fortune. . . .

The autumnal tints grow gradually darker and duller, but not less rich to my eye. And now a hillside near the river exhibits the darkest, crispy reds and browns of every hue, all agreeably blended. At the foot next the meadow, stands a front rank of smoke-like maples bare of leaves, intermixed with yellow birches. Higher up red oaks of various shades of dull red, with yellowish, perhaps black oaks intermixed, and walnuts, now brown, and near the hill top, or rising above the rest, perhaps, a still yellowish oak, and here and there amid the rest or in the foreground on the meadow, dull ashy salmon-colored white oaks large and small, all these contrasting with the clear liquid, sempiternal green of pines.

. . . I stop a while at Cheney's shore to hear an incessant musical twittering from a large flock of young goldfinches which have dull-yellow and drab and black plumage, on maples etc., while the leaves are falling. Young birds can hardly restrain themselves, and if they did not leave us, might perchance burst forth into song in the *later* Indian-summer days.

There are many crisped but colored leaves resting on the smooth surface of the Assabet, which for the most part is not stirred by a breath; but in some places, where the middle is rippled by a slight breeze, no leaves are seen, while the broad and perfectly smooth portions next the shore will be covered with them, as if by a current they were prevented from falling on the other parts. These leaves are chiefly of the red maple, with some white maple, etc. To be sure, they hardly begin to conceal the river, unless in some quiet coves, yet they remind me of ditches in swamps, whose surfaces are often quite concealed by leaves now. The waves made by my boat cause them to rustle, and both by sounds and sights I am reminded that I am in the very midst of the fall. . . .

One reason why I associate perfect reflections from still water with this and a later season may be that by now, by the fall of the leaves, so much more light is let in to the water. The river reflects more light therefore in this twilight of the year, as it were in an afterglow.

The lit river, purling and eddying onward, was spotted with recently fallen leaves, some of which were being carried around by eddies. Leaves are now falling all the country over; some in the swamps, concealing the water; some in woods and on hillsides, where perhaps Vulcan may find them in the spring; some by the wayside, gathered into heaps, where children are playing with them; and some are being conveyed silently seaward on rivers; concealing the water in swamps, where at length they flat out and

sink to the bottom, and we never hear of them again, unless
we shall see their impressions on the coal of a future geological period. Some add them to their manure heaps; others
consume them with fire. The trees repay the earth with
interest for what they have taken from it. The trees are
discounting.

I cannot easily dismiss the subject of the fallen leaves.
How densely they cover and conceal the water for several
feet in width, under and amid the alders and button-bushes
and maples along the shore of the river—still light, tight
and dry boats, dense cities of boats, their fibres not relaxed
by the waters, undulating and rustling with every wave, of
such various pure and delicate, though fading tints—of hues
that might make the fame of teas—dried on Nature's great
coppers. And then see this great fleet of scattered leaf
boats, still tight and dry, each one curled up on every
side by the sun's skill, like boats of hide, scarcely moving
in the sluggish current—like the great fleets with which you
mingle on entering some great mart, some New York which
we are all approaching together. Or else they are slowly
moving around in some great eddy which the river makes,
where the water is deep and the current is wearing into the
bank. How gently each has been deposited on the water!
No violence has been used toward them yet. But next the
shore, as thick as foam they float, and when you turn your
prow that way, list! What a rustling of the crisped waves!

Wood ducks are about now, amid the painted leaves.

October has been the month of autumnal tints. The first
of the month the tints began to be more general, at which
time the frosts began, though there were scattered bright
tints long before; but not until then did the forest begin to
be painted. By the end of the month the leaves will either

have fallen or be sered and turned brown by the frost for the most part.

Yesterday toward night, gave Sophia and mother a sail as far as the Battle Ground. One-eyed John Goodwin, the fisherman, was loading into a handcart and conveying home the piles of driftwood which of late he had collected with his boat. It was a beautiful evening, and a clear amber sunset lit up all the eastern shores; and that man's employment, so simple and direct—though he is regarded by most as a vicious character—whose whole motive was so easy to fathom—thus to obtain his winter's wood—charmed me unspeakably....

Goodwin is a most constant fisherman. He must well know the taste of pickerel by this time. He will fish, I would not venture to say how many days in succession. When I can remember to have seen him fishing almost daily for some time, if it rains, I am surprised on looking out to see him slowly wending his way to the river in his oilcloth coat, with his basket and pole. I saw him the other day fishing in the middle of the stream, the day after I had seen him fishing on the shore, while by a kind of magic I sailed by him; and he said he was catching minnow for bait in the winter. When I was twenty rods off, he held up a pickerel that weighed two and a half pounds, which he had forgot to show me before, and the next morning, as he afterwards told me, he caught one that weighed three pounds. If it is ever necessary to appoint a committee on fish-pounds and pickerel, let him be one of them. Surely he is tenacious of life, hard to scale.

As I am paddling home swiftly before the northwest wind, absorbed in my wooding, I see, this cool and grayish evening, that peculiar yellow light in the east, from the sun a little before its setting. It has just come out beneath a great cold slate-colored cloud that occupies most of the western sky, as smaller ones the eastern, and now its rays, slanting over the hill in whose shadow I float, fall on the eastern trees and hills with a thin yellow light like a clear yellow wine, but somehow it reminds me that now the hearth-side is getting to be a more comfortable place than out-of-doors. Before I get home the sun has set and a cold white light in the west succeeded.

Ground pretty white with frost. The stiffened and frosted weeds and grass have an aggrieved look. The lately free-flowing blades of grass look now like mourning tresses sculptured stiffly in marble; they lie stiff and disheveled. A very narrow strip of ice has formed along the riverside, in which I see a pad or two, wearing the same aggrieved look, like the face of the child that cried for spilt milk, its summer irrevocably gone. Going through the stiff meadow-grass I collect the particles of white frost on the top of my shoes. . . . The black willows along the river are about as bare as in November. The button-bushes are completely bare, letting in more light to the water, and these days I see on their stems the ribbed reflections of the waves I have made. Blackbirds go over chattering, and a small hawk—pigeon or sparrow—glides along and alights on an elm.

As I paddle under the Hemlock bank this cloudy after-noon, about 3 o'clock, I see a screech owl sitting on the edge of a hollow hemlock stump about three feet high, at the base of a large hemlock. It sits with its head drawn in, eyeing me, with its eyes partly open, about twenty feet off. When it hears me move, it turns its head toward me, perhaps one eye only open, with its great glaring golden iris. You see two whitish triangular lines above the eyes meeting at the bill, with a sharp reddish-brown triangle between and a narrow curved line of black under each eye.

At this distance and in this light, you see only a black spot where the eye is, and the question is whether the eyes are open or not. It sits on the lee side of the tree this raw and windy day.

You would say that this was a bird without a neck. Its short bill, which rests upon its breast, scarcely projects at all, but in a state of rest the whole upper part of the bird from the wings is rounded off smoothly, excepting the horns, which stand up conspicuously or are slanted back. After watching it ten minutes from the boat, I landed two rods above, and, stealing quietly up behind the hemlock, though from the windward, I looked carefully around it, and, to my surprise, saw the owl still sitting there. So I sprang round quickly, with my arm outstretched, and caught it in my hand.

It was so surprised that it offered no resistance at first, only glared at me in mute astonishment with eyes as big as saucers. But ere long it began to snap its bill, making quite a noise, and, as I rolled it up in my handkerchief and put it in my pocket, it bit my finger slightly. I soon took it out of my pocket and, tying the handkerchief, left it on the bottom of the boat. So I carried it home and made a small cage in which to keep it for a night. When I took it up, it clung so tightly to my hand as to sink its claws into my fingers and bring blood.

When alarmed or provoked most, it snaps its bill and hisses. It puffs up its feathers to nearly twice its usual size, stretches out its neck, and, with wide-open eyes, stares this way and that, moving its head slowly and undulatingly from side to side with a curious motion. While I write this evening, I see that there is ground for much superstition in it. It looks out on me from a dusky corner of its box with its great solemn eyes, so perfectly still itself. I was surprised to find that I could imitate its note as I remember it, by a *gutteral* whinnering.

A remarkably squat figure, being very broad in proportion to its length, with a short tail, and very cat-like in the face with its horns and great eyes. Remarkably large feet and talons, legs thickly clothed with whitish down, down to the talons. It brought blood from my fingers by clinging to them. It would lower its head, stretch out its neck, and, bending it from side to side, peer at you with laughable circumspection; from side to side, as if to catch or absorb into its eyes every ray of light, strain at you with complacent yet earnest scrutiny. Raising and lowering its head and moving it from side to side in a slow regular manner, at the same time snapping its bill smartly perhaps, and faintly hissing, and puffing itself up more and more—cat-like, turtle-like, both in hissing and swelling. The slowness and gravity, not to say solemnity, of this motion are striking. There plainly is no jesting in this case.

October usually sees the occurrence of a northeast storm—a no'the-easter in old fashioned down-East parlance.

Oct. 25. Rain in the night.
P.M.—By boat to Battle-ground.
A rainy day and easterly wind—an easterly storm. . . .

Oct. 26. Hard rain in the night and almost steady rain through the day, the second day. Wind still easterly or northeasterly. . . .
A driving east or northeast storm. I can see through the drisk[1] only a mile. The river is getting partly over the meadows at last, and my spirits rise with it. . . . A storm is

---

[1] Thoreau's sharp ear had caught this colloquialism when in the previous June he had been down on Cape Cod and had recorded—"A mizzling and rainy day with thick driving fog; a drizzling rain, or 'drisk,' as one called it."—Thus is the American language enriched.

a new, and in some respects more active life in nature. Larger migrating birds make their appearance. They at least sympathize with the movements of the watery element and the winds. I see two great fish hawks (*possibly* blue herons) slowly beating northeast against the storm, by what curious tie circling ever near each other and in the same direction, as if you might expect to find the very motes in the air to be paired; two long undulating wings conveying a feathered body through the misty atmosphere, and this inseparably associated with another planet of the same species. I can just glimpse their undulating lines. . . .

I start up snipes also at Clamshell Meadow. This weather sets the migratory birds in motion and also makes them bolder.

Oct. 27. P.M.—Up river

The third day of steady rain; wind northeast. The river has now risen so far over the meadows that I can just cross Hubbard's Great Meadow in my boat. . . .

I sailed swiftly, standing up and tipping my boat to make a keel of its side, though at first it was hard to keep off a lee shore. I looked for cranberries drifted up on the lee side of the meadows but saw few. It was exciting to feel myself tossed by the dark waves and hear them surge about me. The reign of water now begins, and how it gambols and revels! Waves are its leaves, foam its blossoms. How they run and leap in great droves, deriving new excitement from each other! Schools of porpoises and blackfish are only more animated waves and have acquired the gait and game of the sea itself. The high wind and dashing waves are very inspiriting. . . .

When I turn about, it requires all my strength and skill to push the boat back again. I must keep it pointed directly in the teeth of the wind. If it turns a little, the wind gets the advantage of me and I lose ground. The wind being against the stream makes it rise the faster, and also prevents the driftwood from coming down. . . .

The fall (strictly speaking) is approaching an end in this probably annual northeast storm. Thus the summer winds up its accounts. The Indians, it is said, did not look for winter until the springs were full. Long-continued rain and wind come to settle the accounts of the year, filling the springs for winter. . . . This storm reminds men to put things on a winter footing.

As I sat at the wall-corner high on Conantum, the sky generally covered with continuous cheerless-looking slate-colored clouds, except in the west, I saw, through the hollows of the clouds, here and there the blue appearing. All at once a low-slanted glade of sunlight from one of heaven's west windows behind me fell on the bare gray maples, lighting them up with an incredibly intense and pure white light; then, going out there, it lit up some white birch stems south of the pond, then the gray rocks and the pale reddish young oaks of the lower cliffs, and then the very pale brown meadow-grass, and at last the brilliant white breasts of two ducks, tossing on the agitated surface far off on the pond, which I had not detected before. It was but a transient ray, and there was no sunshine afterward, but the intensity of the light was surprising and impressive, like a halo, a glory in which only the just deserved to live. . . .

I look up and see a male marsh hawk with his clean-cut wings that has just skimmed past above my head—not at all disturbed, only tilting his body a little, now twenty rods off, with a demi-semi-quaver of his wings. He is a very neat flyer.

On the last day of October in the year 1853 there occurred a phenomenon peculiarly characteristic of this season—an abundance of gossamer.

P.M.—By boat with Sophia to my grapes laid down in front
of Fair Haven.

It is a beautiful, warm and calm Indian-summer afternoon.
The river is so high over the meadows, and the pads and
other weeds so deeply buried, and the water is so smooth
and glassy withal, that I am reminded of a calm April day
during the freshets. The coarse withered grass and the
willows and button-bushes with their myriad balls and
whatever else stands on the brink, are reflected with wonderful distinctness. This shore, thus seen from the boat, is like
the ornamented frame of a mirror. The button-balls etc.
are more distinct in the reflection, if I remember, because
they have there for background the reflected sky, but the
actual ones are seen against the russet meadow. I even see
houses a mile off distinctly reflected in the meadow flood.
The cocks crow in barnyards as if with a new lustiness. They
seem to appreciate the day. . . .

I slowly discover that this is a gossamer day. I first see
the fine lines stretching from one weed or grass stem or
rush to another, sometimes seven or eight feet distant,
horizontally and only four or five inches above the water.
When I look further, I find that they are everywhere and on
everything sometimes forming conspicuous fine white gossamer webs on the heads of grasses, or suggesting an Indian
bat. They are so abundant that they seem to have been
suddenly produced in the atmosphere by some chemistry—
spun out of air—I know not for what purpose. I remember
that in Kirby and Spence[2] it is not allowed that the spider
can walk on the water to carry his web across from rush to
rush, but here I see myriads of spiders on the water, making
some kind of progress, and one at least with a line attached

---

[2] Kirby, William and William Spence, *An Introduction to Entomology*,
London, 1856.

This reference is taken from the catalogue of Thoreau's library prepared
by Walter Harding. Since the date of the above entry is October 31, 1853,
it is apparent that Thoreau had access to an earlier edition.

to him. True they do not appear to walk well, but they stand up high and dry on the tips of their toes, and are blown along quite fast. They are of various sizes and colors, though mostly a greenish-brown or else black; some very small.

These gossamer lines are not visible unless between you and the sun. We pass some black willows, now of course quite leafless, and when they are between us and the sun they are so completely covered with these fine cobwebs or lines, mainly parallel to one another, that they make one solid woof, a misty woof, against the sun. They are not drawn taut, but curved downward in the middle, like the rigging of vessels—the ropes which stretch from mast to mast—as if the fleets of a thousand Lilliputian nations were collected one behind another under bare poles. But when we have floated a few feet further, and thrown the willow out of the sun's range, not a thread can be seen on it.

I landed and walked up and down the causeway and found it the same there, the gossamer reaching across the causeway, though not necessarily supported on the other side. They streamed southward with the slight zephyr. As if the year were weaving her shroud out of light. It seemed only necessary that the insect have a *point d'appui;* and then, wherever you stood and brought the leeward side of its resting-place between you and the sun, this magic appeared. They were streaming in like manner southward from the railing of the bridge, parallel waving threads of light, producing a sort of flashing in the air. You saw five or six feet in length from one position, but when I moved one side I saw as much more, and found that a great many, at least reached quite across the bridge from side to side, though it was mere accident whether they caught there— though they were continually broken by unconscious travelers. Most indeed were slanted slightly upward, rising about one foot in going four, and in like manner, they were streaming from the south rail over the water. I know not how far. And there were spiders on the rail that produced them, similar to those on the water. Fifteen rods off up the road, beyond the bridge, they looked like a shimmering in the air in the bare tree-tops, the finest, thinnest gossamer veil to the sun, a dim wall.

I am at a loss to say what purpose they serve, and am inclined to think they are to some extent attached to objects as they float through the atmosphere; for I noticed before I had gone far, that my grape-vines in a basket in the boat had got similar lines stretching from one twig to another, a foot or two, having undoubtedly caught them as we paddled along. It might well be an electric phenomenon. The air appeared crowded with them. It was a wonder they did not get into the mouth and nostrils, or that we did not feel them on our faces, or continually going or coming amid them did not whiten our clothes more.

And yet one with his back to the sun, walking the other way, would observe nothing of all this. Only stand so as to bring the south side of any tree, bush, fence, or other object between you and the sun. Methinks it is only on these very finest days late in autumn that this phenomenon is seen, as if that fine vapor of the morning were spun into these webs.[3]

---

[3] Of the several kinds of silk that spiders spin out of the spinnerets located outside their abdomens, one is known as the drag-line. It is upon this thin filament that they descend and ascend, oftentimes apparently in thin air, the tenuous strand being invisible. See *The Spider Book* by John Henry Comstock, New York, 1912. It is believed that spiders are transported through the air when these minute wavering strands are torn loose from their delicate moorings and are borne on a breeze. Gossamer is a great quantity of such, floating through the air loose, or attached to some physical object. The derivation of the term is obscure. It has been suggested that the word goose in involved, referring to the downy appearance of gossamer, or else to its prevalence when geese are in the air. "Gossamer, methinks," recorded Thoreau on November 15, 1858, "belongs to the latter part of October and the first part of November."

October is the month of painted leaves, of ripe leaves, when all the earth, not merely flowers, but fruits and leaves are ripe. With respect to its colors and its seasons, it is the sunset month of the year, when the earth is painted like a sunset sky. This rich glow flashes round the world. This light fades into the clear, white, leafless twilight of November, and whatever more glowing sunset or Indian summer we have then is the afterglow of the year.

November

November—the month of withered leaves and bare twigs and limbs.

This is the month of nuts and nutty thoughts—that November whose name sounds so bleak and cheerless. Perhaps its harvest of thought is worth more than all the other crops of the year. Men are more serious now.

It is a pleasant day but breezy, and now I can hardly detect any gossamer left on the willows. This wind, per-chance, shaking the willows and the reeds—shaking and bending their masts—strains and breaks this fine cordage, and, moreover the spiders cannot well walk on the surface of the water now. So it would seem, it must not only be a perfectly fair Indian-summer day, but quite calm and the water smooth, to permit of this wonderful display and, perchance, after one of those remarkable and memorable mornings when the air is peculiarly clear and resonant and that white vapor as of frost-steam hangs over the earth—after a clear, cool calm Indian-summer morning in November. And must it not always follow the fall of the leaf when there is least motion to the twigs. The short time in which it must be produced and for which it endures, is remarkable.

P.M.—Up Assabet, a-wooding.

. . . The river is perfectly smooth. Whole schools of *little* minnows leap from the surface at once with a silvery gleam. The wool grass with its drooping head and the slender withered leaves dangling about its stem, stands in little sheaves upon its tussocks, clean dry straw, and is thus reflected in the water. This is the November shore. . . .

As I pushed up the river past Hildreth's, I saw the blue heron arise from the shore and disappear with heavily-flapping wings around a bend in front; the greatest of the bitterns—*Ardeae*—with heavily undulating wings, low over the water, seen against the woods, just disappearing round a bend in front; with a great slate-colored expanse of wing, suited to the shadows of the stream, a tempered blue as of the sky and dark water commingled.

This is the aspect under which the Musketaquid might be represented at this season: a long, smooth lake, reflecting the bare willows and button-bushes, the stubble and the wool-grass on its tussock, a muskrat-cabin or two conspicuous on its margin amid the unsightly tops of pontederia, and a bittern disappearing on undulating wing around a bend.

On the 1st, when I stood on Poplar Hill, I saw a man, far off by the edge of the river, splitting billets off a stump. Suspecting who it was, I took out my glass, and beheld

Goodwin, the one-eyed Ajax, in his short blue frock, short and square-bodied, as broad as for his height he can afford to be, getting his winter's wood; for this is one of the phenomena of the season. As surely as the ants which he disturbs go into winter quarters in the stump when the weather becomes cool, so does G. revisit the stumpy shores with his axe. As usual, his powder-flask peeped out from a pocket on his breast, his gun was slanted over a stump near by, and his boat lay a little further along. He had been at work laying wall[1] still further off, and now, near the end of the day, betook himself to those pursuits which he loved better still. . . .

But, strange to say, the town does not like to have him get his fuel in this way. They would rather the stumps would rot in the ground, or be floated downstream to the sea. They have almost without dissent agreed on a different mode of living, with their division of labor. They would have him stick to laying wall, and buy corded wood for his fuel, as they do. He has drawn up an old bridge sleeper and cut his name in it for security, and now he gets into his boat and pushes off in the twilight, saying he will go and see what Mr. Musquash is about.

I look westward across Fair Haven Pond. The warmer colors are now rare. A cool and silvery light is the prevailing one; dark-blue or slate-colored clouds in the west, and the sun going down in them. All the light of November may be called an afterglow.

Climbed the wooded hill by Holden's spruce swamp and got a novel view of the river and Fair Haven Bay through the almost leafless woods. How much handsomer a river or lake such as ours, seen thus through a foreground of

---

[1] *I.e.*, building a stone wall.

scattered or else partially leafless trees, though at a considerable distance this side of it, especially if the water is
open without wooded shores or isles! It is the most perfect
and beautiful of all frames which yet the sketcher is commonly careful to brush aside. I mean a pretty thick foreground, a view of the distant water through the near forest,
through a thousand little vistas, as we are rushing toward
the former—that intimate mingling of wood and water
which excites an expectation which the near and open view
rarely realizes. We prefer that some part be concealed which
our imagination may navigate.

To Conantum by boat, nutting.

October 31st when the river was at its height after the
rains of the 24th and 28th, our first fall flood, the wreck
of the river and meadow with an unusual quantity of
cranberries was washed up, and is now left high and dry,
forming the first water-mark of the season, an endless
meandering light-brown line, further from or nearer to the
river. It is now very fresh, and it is comparatively easy to
distinguish the materials which compose it. But I love to
see it even in mid-summer, the old water-line of the last
year, far away from the edge of the shrunken stream in some
meadow, perchance in the woods, reminding me of the floods
and the windy days of the fall and spring, of ducks and
geese and gulls, of the raw and gusty days which I have
spent on the then wilderness of water, of the origin of
things, as it were, when water was a prevailing element.
The flood comes and takes all the summer's waste, all that
lies loose, from the riverside and meadows and floats it,
not to ocean, but as far toward the upland as the water
reaches; there it plants again and again the seeds of
fluviatile shrubs and trees and flowers. A new line of
wreckage is formed every year. . . .

Under the warm south side of Bittern Cliff, where I

moor my boat, I hear one cricket singing loudly and undauntedly still, in the warm rockside.

I shook two mocker-nut trees; one just ready to drop its nuts[2] and most came out of the shells. But the other tree was not ready; only a part fell, and those mostly in the shells. This is the time for our best walnuts; the smallest say the last of October. Got a peck and a half shelled. I did not wish to slight any of Nature's gifts. I am partial to the peculiar and wholesome sweetness of a nut, and I think that some time is profitably spent every autumn in gathering even such as our pignuts. Some of them are very sizable, rich-looking and palatable fruit. How can we expect to understand Nature unless we accept like children these her smallest gifts, valuing them more as her gifts than for their intrinsic value? I love to get my basket full, however small and comparatively worthless the nut. It takes very severe frosts, and sun and wind thereafter, to kill and open the shells so that the nuts will drop out. Many hold on all winter. . . .

The shallow pools in woods were skimmed over this morning, and there was a little ice along the riverside which can still be detected at sundown. Three bluebirds still braving the cold winds—Acton Blues, not gone into winter quarters. Their blue uniform makes me think of soldiers who have received orders to keep the field and not go into winter quarters.

Rounding the Island just after sunset. I see not only the houses nearest the river but our own reflected in the river by the Island. From what various points of view and in what unsuspected lights and relations we sooner or later see the most familiar objects! I see houses reflected in the

---

[2] This is the nut of the smooth-barked North American hickory, *Carya alba*.

river which stand a mile from it, and whose inhabitants do not consider themselves near the shore.

The reflections in the river fascinated Thoreau and they receive frequent comment in the Journal, particularly at this time of the year. It was his view that "It is only a reflecting mind that sees reflections," and he wrote that "In the reflection you have an infinite number of eyes to see for you and report the aspect of things each from its point of view."

Returning, I see the red oak on R.W.E.'s shore reflected in the bright sky water. In the reflection the tree is black against the clear whitish sky, though as I see it against the opposite woods it is a warm greenish yellow. But the river sees it against the bright sky, and hence the reflection is like ink. The water tells me how it looks to it seen from below.

The river was perfectly smooth except the upwelling of its tide, and as we paddled home westward, the dusky yellowing sky was all reflected in it, together with the dun-colored clouds and the trees, and there was more light in the water than in the sky. The reflections of the trees and bushes on the banks were wonderfully dark and distinct, for though frequently we could not see the real bush in the twilight against the dark bank, in the water it appeared against the sky. We were thus often enabled to steer clear of the over-hanging bushes.

P.M.—To Cardinal Shore.

Going over Swamp Bridge Brook at 3 P.M. I saw in the pond by the roadside a few rods before me, the sun shining bright, a mink swimming, the whole length of his back out. It was a rich brown fur, glowing internally as the sun fell

on it, like some ladies' boas, not black, as it sometimes
appears, especially on ice. It landed within three rods, showing its long, somewhat cat-like neck, and I observed was
carrying something by its mouth, dragging it overland. At
first I thought it a fish, maybe an eel, and when it had got
half a dozen feet, I ran forward, and it dropped its prey and
went into the wall. It was a muskrat, the head and part of
the fore legs torn off and gone, but the rest still fresh and
quite heavy, including hind legs and tail. It had probably
killed this muskrat in the brook, eaten so much, and was
dragging the remainder to its retreat in the wall.

Saw sixty geese go over the Great Fields, in one waving
line broken from time to time by their crowding on each
other and vainly endeavoring to form into a harrow, honking
all the while.

The air is full of geese. I saw five flocks within an hour
about 10 A.M. containing from thirty to fifty each, and
afterward two more flocks, making in all from two hundred
and fifty to three hundred at least, all flying southwest over
Goose and Walden Ponds. . . . According to my calculation
a thousand or fifteen hundred may have gone over Concord
today.

*The flight of wild geese was a harbinger of a change in the
weather in both the spring of the year and the fall, Thoreau
writing on the 20th of November, 1853—"Methinks the
geese are wont to go south just before a storm, and, in the
spring, to go north just after one, say at the end of a long
April storm."*

High wind and rain in the night. Still more strong and
gusty but remarkably warm southwest wind during the day.
P.M. To Fair Haven Hill by boat with W.E.C.
We rowed against a very powerful wind, sometimes

scarcely making any headway. It was with difficulty often that we moved our paddles through the air for a new stroke. As C. said, it seemed to blow out of a hole. We had to turn our oars edgewise to it. But we worked our way slowly upward nevertheless, for we came to feel and hear it blow and see the waves run. There was quite a sea running on the lee shore—broad black waves with white crests, which made our boat toss very pleasantly. They wet the piers of the railroad bridge for eighteen inches up. I should guess that the whole height from the valley between the top of a wave was nearer to fifteen inches. . . .

Landed and walked over Conant's Indian rye-field, and I picked up two good arrowheads. The river with its waves has a very wild look southward, and I see the white caps of the waves in Fair Haven Bay. Went into the woods by Holden Swamp and sat down to hear the wind roar amid the tree-tops. What an incessant straining of the trees. It is a music that wears better than the opera, methinks. This reminds me how the telegraph wire hummed coarsely in the tempest as we passed under it.

Hitherto it had only rained a little from time to time, but now it began to rain in earnest. We hastily rowed across to the firm ground of Fair Haven Hillside, drew up our boat and turned it over in a twinkling on to a clump of alders covered with cat-briars which kept up the lee side, and crawled under it. There we lay half an hour on the damp ground and cat-briars, hardly able to see out to the storm which we heard on our roof, through the thick alder stems, much pleased with the tightness of our roof which we frequently remarked upon. We took immense satisfaction in the thoroughness of the protection against the rain which it afforded. . . . At length as it threatened to be an all-night storm, we crawled out again and set sail homeward.

It now began to rain harder than ever, and the wind was so strong and gusty, and blew so nearly at right angles with the river, that we found it impossible to keep the stream long at a time with our sail set, sitting on one side till the water came in plentifully, that the side might act as a keel, but were repeatedly driven ashore amid the button-bushes, and then had to work our way to the other side slowly and start again. What with water in the boat and in our clothes, we were now indifferent to wet. At length it began to rain so much harder than before, the great drops seeming to flat down the waves and suppress the wind, and feeling like hail on our hands and faces, as we remembered, it had only sprinkled before. By this time of course we were wet quite through and through and C. began to inquire and jest about the condition of our money—a singular prudence methought—and buried his wallet in his pocket-handker-chief and returned it to his pocket again. He thought that bank-bills would be spoiled. It had never occurred to me if a man got completely wet through how it might affect the banknotes in his wallet, it is so rare a thing for me to have any there. At length we both took to rowing vigor-ously to keep ourselves warm and so got home just after candlelight.

Saw in the pool at the Hemlocks what I at first thought was a bright leaf moved by the zephyr on the surface of the smooth dark water, but it was a splendid male summer duck, which allowed us to approach within seven or eight rods, sailing up close to the shore, and then rose and flew up the curving stream. We soon overhauled it again, and got a fair and long view of it. It was a splendid bird, a perfect floating gem, and Blake,[3] who had never seen the

---

[3] Harrison Gray Otis Blake of Worcester, who had been Thoreau's friend and correspondent since 1848, was his companion on many an excursion, notably those in the summer of 1858 on Mount Monadnack and in the White Mountains.

The summer duck is that exquisitely iridescent creature—the wood duck, *Aix sponsa*.

like, was greatly surprised, not knowing that so splendid a bird was found in this part of the world. There it was, constantly moving back and forth by invisible means and wheeling on the smooth surface, showing now its breast, now its side, now its rear. . . .

What an ornament to a river to see that glowing gem floating in contact with its waters! As if the hummingbird should recline its ruby throat and its breast on the water. Like dipping a glowing goal in water! . . .

That duck was all jewels combined, showing different lustres as it turned on the unrippled element in various lights, now brilliant glossy green, now dusky violet, now a rich bronze, now the reflections that sleep in the ruby's grain.

6.30 P.M.—To Baker Farm by boat.

It is full moon and a clear night with a strong northwest wind; so C. and I must have a sail by moonlight. The river has risen surprisingly to a spring height, owing to yesterday's rain, higher than before since spring. We sail rapidly upward. The river apparently, almost actually, as broad as the Hudson. Venus remarkably bright, just ready to set. Not a cloud in the sky, only the moon and a few faint unobtrusive stars here and there, and from time to time a meteor. The water washes against our bows with the same sound that one hears against a vessel's prow by night on the ocean. If you had waked up here, you would not know at first but you were there. The shore-lines are concealed; you look seemingly over an almost boundless waste of waters on either hand. The hills are dark, vast, lumpish. Some near, familiar hill appears as a distant bold mountain, for its base is infinitely removed. It is very pleasant to make our way thus rapidly but mysteriously over the black waves, black as ink and dotted with round foam spots with a long moonlight sheen on one side—to make one's way upward thus over a waste of waters, not knowing where you are exactly, only avoiding shores. The stars are few and faint in this bright light. How well they wear! C. thought a man could still get along with *them* who was considerably reduced in his circumstances, that they were a kind of bread and cheese that never failed.

Fair Haven Hill never looked more grand and mountain-like than now that all its side is dark and we only see its bold outline at an indefinite distance. Under the lee of the Holden wood we found unexpectedly smooth and pleasant water and stillness, where we heard the wind roar behind us. The night is cool but not damp, and methinks you can be abroad with more impunity than in summer nights even. The walls on Conantum are merely black streaks, inky lines running over the hill. The wind goes down somewhat. The features of the landscape are simpler and lumped. We have the moon with a few stars above, a waste of black, dashing waves around, reflecting the moon's sheen on one side, and the distant shore in dark swelling masses, dark floating isles between the water and the sky, on either hand. Moored our boat under Fair Haven Hill.

This evening at sundown when I was on the water, I heard come booming up the river what I suppose was the sound of cannon fired in Lowell to celebrate the Whig victory, the voting down the new Constitution.[4] Perchance no one else in Concord heard them, and it is remarkable that I heard them, who was only interested in the natural

---

[4] On Tuesday morning, the 15th of November, 1853, the *Daily Advertiser* in Lowell carried the following squib:

Terminated, yesterday, in a very unsatisfactory manner to everyone, except those who were expecting defeat and found that their opponents were as badly beaten as themselves. There was no choice for represen- tatives. The whole number of votes cast was 3,956, necessary for a choice 1,979. The highest on the Whig ticket was James Townsend, 1,815; the lowest, Daniel Ayer, 1,747. The new Constitution was re- jected in this city by 138 majority.

phenomenon of sound borne far over the water. The river is now so full and so high over the meadows, and at that hour was so smooth withal, that perchance the waves of sound flowed over the smooth surface of the water with less obstruction and further than in any other direction.

I think it must have been a fish hawk which I saw hovering over the meadow and my boat (a raw cloudy afternoon) now and then sustaining itself in one place a hundred feet or more above the water, intent on a fish, with a hovering or fluttering motion of the wings somewhat like a kingfisher. Its wings were very long, slender and curved in outline of front edge. I think there was some white on rump. It alighted near the top of an oak within rifle-shot of me and my boat, afterward on the tip-top of a maple waterside, looking very large.

I am surprised to see a stake-driver fly up from the weeds within a stone's throw of my boat's place. It drops its excrement from thirty feet in the air, and this falling, one part being heavier than another, takes the form of a snake, and suggests that this may be the origin of some of the stories of this bird swallowing a snake or eel which passed through it.

A cold, gray day, once spitting snow. Water froze in tubs enough to bear last night.

As I go up the meadow-side toward Clamshell, I see a very great collection of crows far and wide on the meadows, evidently gathered by this cold and blustering weather. Probably the moist meadows where they feed are frozen up against them. They flit before me in countless numbers flying very low on account of the strong northwest wind that comes over the hill, and a cold gleam is reflected from the back and wings of each, as from a weather-stained shingle. Some perch within three or four rods of me and seem weary. I see where they have been pecking the apples by the meadow-side. An immense cohort of cawing crows which sudden winter has driven near to the habitations of man. When I return after sunset I see them collecting and hovering over and settling in the dense pine woods west of E. Woods, as if about to roost there.

I find my best way of getting cranberries is to go forth in time of flood, just before the water begins to fall and after strong winds, and, choosing the thickest places, let one, with an instrument like a large coarse dung-fork, hold down the floating grass and other coarser part of the wreck mixed with [it] while another, with a common garden rake, rakes them into the boat, there being just enough chaff left to enable you to get them into the boat, yet with little water.

When I got them home, I filled a half-bushel basket a quarter full and set it in a tub of water, and, stirring the cranberries the coarser part of the chaff was held beneath by the berries rising to the top. Then, raising the basket, draining it, and upsetting it into a bread-trough, the main part of the chaff fell uppermost and was cast aside. Then, draining off the water, I jarred the cranberries alternately to this end and then to that of the trough, each time removing the fine chaff—cranberry leaves and bits of grass—which adhered to the bottom, on the principle of gold washing, except that the gold was what was thrown away, and finally I spread and dried and winnowed them. It would have been better if the basket had been a very coarse riddle and the trough had had a rough bottom.[5]

---

[5] A riddle is a coarse, meshed sieve. Twelve days later Thoreau inserted the following parenthetical note in his *Journal* on December 3, 1853:

(I sent two and a half bushels of my cranberries to Boston and got four dollars for them.)

I was paddling along slowly, on the lookout for what was to be seen, when my attention was caught by a strange-looking leaf or bunch of leaves on the shore, close to the water's edge, a rod distant. I thought to myself, I may as well investigate that, and so pushed slowly toward it, my eyes resting on it all the while. It then looked like a small shipwrecked hulk and, strange to say, like the bare skeleton of a fowl that has been picked and turned yellowish, resting on its breast-bone, the color of a withered black or red oak leaf. Again I thought it must be such a leaf or cluster of leaves peculiarly curved and cut or torn on the upper edges. . . .

Then, all at once, I saw that it was a woodcock, perfectly still, with its head drawn in, standing on its great pink feet. I had, apparently, noticed only the yellowish-brown portions of the plumage, refering the dark-brown to the shore behind it. May it not be that the yellowish-brown markings of the bird corresponded somewhat to its skeleton? At any rate with my eye steadily on it from a point within a rod, I did not for a considerable time suspect it to be a living creature. Examining the shore after it had flown with a whistling flight, I saw that there was a clear space of mud between the water and the edge of ice-crystals about two inches wide, melted so far by the lapse of the water, and all along the edge of the ice, for a rod or two at least, there was a hole where it had thrust its bill down, probing, every half-inch, frequently closer. Some animal life must be collected at that depth just in that narow space, savory morsels for this bird.

The chubby bird dashed away zigzag, carrying its long tongue-case carefully before it, over the witch-hazel bushes. This is its walk—the portion of the shore, the narrow strip, still kept open and unfrozen between the water's edge and the ice. The sportsman might discover its neighborhood by these probings.

I found Fair Haven skimmed entirely over though the stones which I threw down on it from the high bank on the east broke through. Yet the river was open. The landscape looked singularly clean and pure and dry, the air, like a pure glass, being laid over the picture, the trees so tidy, stripped of their leaves; the meadows and pastures, clothed with clean dry grass, looked as if they had been swept; ice on the water and winter in the air, but yet not a particle of snow on the ground. The woods divested in great part of their leaves, are being ventilated. It is the season of perfect works, of hard, tough, ripe twigs, not of tender buds and leaves. The leaves have made their wood, and a myriad new withes stand up all around pointing to the sky, able to survive the cold. It is only the perennial that you see, the iron age of the year.

These expansions of the river skim over before the river itself takes on its icy fetters. What is the analogy?

I saw a muskrat come out of a hole in the ice. He is a man wilder than Ray or Melvin. While I am looking at him, I am thinking what he is thinking of me. He is a different sort of man, that is all. He would dive when I went nearer then reappear again, and had kept open a place five or six feet square so that it had not frozen, by swimming about in it. Then he would sit on the edge of the ice and busy himself about something, I could not see whether it was a clam or not. What a cold-blooded fellow! thoughts at a low temperature, sitting perfectly still so long on ice covered with water, mumbling a cold, wet clam in its shell.

Geese went over on the 13th and 14th, on the 17th the first snow fell, and on the 19th it began to be cold and blustering.

A clear, cold, windy day. The water on the meadows, which are rapidly becoming bare, is skimmed over and reflects a whitish light like silver plating, while the un-frozen river is a dark blue.

It is too cold today to use a paddle; the water freezes on the handle and numbs my fingers.

It is remarkable how much power I can exert through the undulations which I produce by rocking my boat in the middle of the river. Some time after I have ceased I am surprised to hear the sound of the undulations which have just reached the shores acting on the thin ice there and making a complete wreck of it for a long distance up and down the stream, cracking off pieces four feet wide and more. I have stirred up the river to do this work, a power which I cannot put to rest.

November 29th, walked in P.M. to old stone bridge and down bank of river by Sam Barrett's house.

When I stood on the caving swallow banks by the bridge about 4 o'clock, the sun sank below some clouds, or they rose above it, and it shone out with that bright, calm, memorable light which I have elsewhere described, lighting up the pitch pines and everything. The patches of winter rye, at this season so green by contrast, are an interesting feature in the landscape. When I got out of the wood, going toward Barrett's, the softness of the sunlight on the russet landscape, the smooth russet grassy fields and mead-ows, was very soothing, the sun now getting low in a No-vember day. The stems and twigs of the maples, etc., looking down the river, were beautifully distinct. You see distinctly the form of the various clumps of maples and birches. Geese in river swam as fast as I walked.

Nov. 30. River skimmed over behind Dodd's and else-where. Got in my boat. River remained iced over all day. . . .

On the 27th, when I made my last voyage for the season, I found a large sound pine log about four feet long floating, and brought it home. Off the larger end I sawed two wheels, about a foot in diameter and seven or eight inches thick, and I fitted to them an axle-tree of a joist, which also I found in the river, and thus I had a convenient pair of wheels on which to get my boat up and roll it about.

The assessors called me into their office this year and said they wished to get an inventory of my property; asked if I had any real estate. No. Any notes at interest or railroad shares? No. Any taxable property? None that I know of.

"I own a boat," I said.

And one of them thought that that might come under the head of a pleasure carriage, which is taxable. Now that I have wheels to it, it comes nearer to it. I was pleased to get my boat in by this means rather than on a borrowed wheel-barrow. It was fit that the river should furnish the material, and that in my last voyage on it, when the ice reminded me that it was time to put it in winter quarters.[6]

The river may be said to have frozen generally last night.

---

[6] This entry appears on the last day of November in the year 1855. Five years later on the 29th of the month, Thoreau wrote:

"Get up my boat, 7 A.M. Thin ice of the night is floating down the river."

This simple factual statement was his last record of the Concord River. Four days later while engaged in measuring some white oaks and counting the rings of a felled hickory, he caught a severe cold which, as he wrote his friend Ricketson in the following March, "resulted in a kind of bronchitis, so that I have been confined to the house ever since."

It was the beginning of the end. Thoreau died of tuberculosis at the age of forty-four on May 6, 1862.

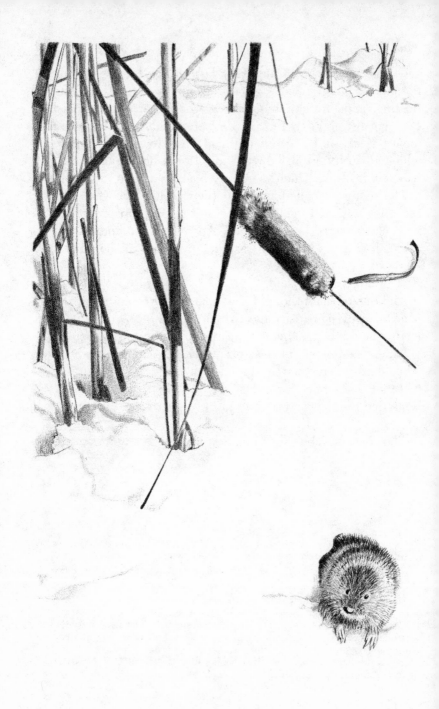

Winter

I love to have the river closed up for a season and a pause put to my boating, to be obliged to get my boat in. I shall launch it again in the spring with so much more pleasure. This is an advantage in point of abstinence and moderation compared with the seaside boating, where the boat ever lies on the shore. I love best to have each thing in its season only, and enjoy doing without it at all other times.

In the decade of regular daily entries in Thoreau's Journal *(1851-61), the only record of his boating on the river in the month of December is in the years 1852 and 1853. Thus on the 2nd of December, 1852 he recorded—"I do not remember when I have taken a sail or a row on the river in December before."*

Here in The River *the seasons have been arbitrarily marked off by the dates of the two equinoxes—vernal and autumnal—and the summer solstice. In the spring of every year save 1852 and 1856 Thoreau, during the third week*

of March, launched his boat into "that element from which
[he wrote] I have been debarred for three months and a
half." In keeping with this pattern and with the stark
reality of a New England winter, this season starts here
with the first of December.

7 A.M.—How can we spare to be abroad in the morning
red, to see the forms of the leafless eastern trees against
the dun sky and hear the cocks crow, when a thin, low mist
hangs over the ice and frost in meadows? I have come
along the riverside in Merrick's pasture to collect for kindling
the fat pine roots and knots which the spearers dropped last
spring and which the floods have washed up. Get a heaping
bushel-basketful. The thin, trembling sheets of imperfectly
cemented ice or ice-crystals, loosened by the warmth of the
day, now go floating down the stream, looking like dark
ripples in the twilight and grating against the edges of the
firm ice. They completely fill the river where it is bridged
with firmer ice below.

The river meadows where they were not cut, are conspicuous brown-straw-colored now—in the sun almost a true
straw-color. November lingers still there.

Ceased raining and mizzling last evening, and cleared off,
with a high northwest wind, which shook the house, coming
in fitful gusts, but only they who slept on the west sides of
houses knew of it.

7.30 A.M.—Take a run down the riverside. . . .

Dark waves are chasing each other across the river from
northwest to southeast and breaking the edge of the snow
ice which has formed for half a rod in width along the
edge, and the fragments of broken ice, what arctic voyagers
call "brash," carry forward the undulation. I am pleased
to see from afar the highest water-mark of a spring freshet

on Cheney's boat-house, a level light-colored mark about an inch wide running the whole length of the building, now several years old, where probably a thin ice chafed it. . . .

Smooth white reaches of ice, as long as the river on each side are threatening to bridge over its dark-blue artery any night. They remind me of a trap that is set for it, which the frost will spring. Each day at present, the wriggling river nibbles off the edges of the trap which have advanced in the night.[1] It is a close contest between day and night, heat and cold.

A still, completely gray, overcast, chilly morning. At 8.30 a fine snow begins to fall, increasing very gradually, perfectly straight down, till in fifteen minutes the ground is white, the smooth places first, and thus the winter landscape is ushered in. And now it is falling thus all the land over, sifting down through the tree-tops in the woods, and on the meadow and pastures, where the dry grass and weeds conceal it at first, and on the river and ponds, in which it is dissolved. But in a few minutes it turns to rain, and so the wintry landscape is postponed for the present.

We have now the scenery of winter, though the snow is but an inch or two deep. . . . Ah, who can tell the serenity and clarity of a New England winter sunset? This could not be till the cold and the snow came. Ah, what isles those western clouds! In what a sea! Just after sunset there is a broad pillar of light for many minutes in the west.

We are tempted to call these the finest days of the year. Take Fair Haven Pond, for instance, a perfectly level plain of white snow, untrodden as yet by any fisherman, surrounded by snow-clad hills, dark evergreen woods, and red-

---

[1] The next day the *Journal* records—"The ice trap was sprung last night."

dish oak leaves, so pure and still. The last rays of the sun falling on Baker Farm reflect a clear pink color.

P.M.—With C. up north bank of Assabet to bridge.

Good sleighing still, with but little snow. A warm, thawing day. The river is open almost its whole length. It is a beautifully smooth mirror within an icy frame. It is well to improve such a time to walk by it. This strip of water of irregular width over the channel, between broad fields of ice, looks like a polished silver mirror, or like another surface of polished ice, and often is distinguished from the surrounding ice only by its reflections. I have rarely seen any reflections—of weeds, willows and elms, and the houses of the village—so distinct, the stems so black and distinct; for they contrast not with a green meadow but clear white ice, to say nothing of the silvery surface of the water.

Your eye slides first over a plane surface of smooth ice of one color to a water surface of silvery smoothness, like a gem set in ice, and reflecting the weeds and trees and houses and clouds with singular beauty. The reflections are particularly simple and distinct. These twigs are not referred to and confounded with a broad green meadow from which they spring, as in summer, but, instead of that dark-green ground, absorbing the light is this abrupt white field of ice.

On river to Fair Haven Pond.

My first true winter walk is perhaps that which I take on the river, or where I cannot go in the summer. It is the walk peculiar to winter, and now first I take it. I see that the fox too has already taken the same walk before me, just along the edge of the button-bushes, where not even he can go in the summer. We both turn our steps hither at the same time.

There is now, at 2.30 P.M., the melon-rind arrangement of

the clouds. Really parallel columns of fine mackerel sky, reaching quite across the heavens from west to east, with clear intervals of blue sky, and a fine-grained vapor like spun glass extending in the same direction beneath the former. In half an hour all this mackerel sky is gone. What an ever-changing scene is the sky with its drifting cirrhus and stratus! . . .

Now that the river is frozen we have a sky under our feet also. Going over black ice three or four inches thick, only reassured by seeing the thickness at the cracks, I see it richly marked internally with large whitish figures suggesting rosettes of ostrich feathers or coral. These at first appear to be a dust on the surface, but looking closely, are found to be at various angles with it internally, in the grain. The work of crystallization. Often you see as it were a sheaf of feathered arrows five or six feet long, very delicate but perfectly straight, their planes make a very slight angle with the surface of the ice, and yet no seam is to be detected. The black floor is by these divided into polygonal segments for the most part geometrically straight-sided. Their position merely suggests a cleavage which has no existence. Perhaps it is the angle of excidence answering to the angle of incidence at which the sun's light and heat strikes the ice at different hours!!

I walk thus along the riverside, perhaps between the button-bushes and the meadow, where the bleached and withered grass—the *Panicum virgatum* and blue-joint and wool-grass—rustle amid the osiers which have saved them from the scythe. When the snow is only thus deep, the yellowish straw color of the sedge in the meadows rising above the snow is now first appreciated, seen between the ice and the snow-clad land.

Twice this winter I have noticed a musquash floating in a placid open place in the river when it was frozen for a mile each side, looking at first like a bit of stump or frozen meadow, but showing its whole upper outline from nose to end of tail; perfectly still till he observed me, then suddenly diving and steering under the ice toward some cabin's entrance or other retreat half a dozen rods or more off.

What a different phenomenon a musquash now from what it is in summer! Now if one floats, or swims, its whole back out, or crawls out upon the ice at one of those narrow oval water spaces in the river, some twenty rods long (in calm weather, smooth mirrors) in a broad frame of white ice or yet whiter snow, it is seen at once, as conspicuous (or more so) as a fly on a window pane or a mirror. But in summer, how many hundreds crawl along the weedy shore or plunge in the long river unsuspected by the boatman! Even if the musquash is not there I often see the open clamshell on the edge of the ice, perfectly distinct a long way off, and he is betrayed.

Some of the clamshells, freshly opened by the muskrats and left lying on their half sunken cabins, where they are kept wet by the waves, show very handsome rainbow tints. . . . It is a somewhat saddening reflection that the beautiful colors of this shell for want of light cannot be said to exist, until its inhabitant has fallen a prey to the spoiler, and it is thus left a wreck on the strand. Its beauty then beams forth, and it remains a splendid cenotaph to its departed tenant, symbolical of those radiant realms of light to which the latter has risen—what glory he has gone to.

Just this side of Bittern Cliff, I see a very remarkable track of an otter, made undoubtedly December 3d, when this snow ice was mere slosh. It had come up through a hole (now black ice) by the stem of a button-bush, and, apparently, pushed its way through the slosh, as through snow on land, leaving a track eight inches wide, more or less, with the now frozen snow shoved up two inches high on each side *i.e.* two inches above the general level. Where the ice was firmer are seen only the tracks of its feet. It had crossed the open middle (now thin black ice) and continued its singular trail to the opposite shore, as if a narrow sled had been drawn bottom upward.

At Bittern Cliff I saw where they had been playing, sliding, or fishing, apparently today, on the snow-covered rocks on which, for a rod upward and as much in width, the snow was trodden and worn quite smooth, as if twenty had trodden and slid there for several hours. Their droppings are a mass of fishes' scales and bones—loose scaly, black masses. At this point the black ice approached within three or four feet of the rock, and there was an open space just there, a foot or two across, which appeared to have been kept open by them. I continued along up that side and crossed on white ice just below the pond. The river was all tracked up with otters from Bittern Cliff upward.

Sunday P.M.—Take my first skate to Fair Haven Pond.
It takes my feet a few moments to get used to the skates. I see the track of one skater who has preceded me this morning. This is the first skating. I keep mostly to the smooth ice about a rod wide next the shore commonly, where there was an overflow a day or two ago. There is not the slightest overflow today, and yet it is warm (thermometer at 25 at 4.30 P.M.). It must be that the river is falling. Now I go shaking over hobbly places, now shoot over a bridge of ice only a foot wide between the water and the shore at a bend—Hubbard Bath—always so at first there. Now I suddenly see the trembling surface of water where I thought were black spots of ice around me.

The river is rather low, so that I cannot keep the river

above the Clamshell Bend. I am confined to a very narrow edging of ice in the meadow, gliding with unexpected ease through withered sedge, but slipping sometimes on a twig; again taking to the snow to reach the next ice, but this rests my feet; straddling the bare black willows, winding between the button-bushes, and following narrow thread-ings of ice amid the sedge, which bring me out to clear fields unexpectedly. Occasionally I am obliged to take a few strokes over black and thin-looking ice, where the neighbor-ing bank is springy, and am slow to acquire confidence in it, but, returning, how bold I was! Where the meadow seemed only sedge and snow, I find a complete ice con-nection.

At Cardinal Shore, as usual, there is a great crescent of hobbly ice, where two or three days ago, the northwest wind drove the waves back up-stream and broke up the edge of the ice. This crescent is eight or ten rods wide and twice as many long, and consists of cakes of ice from a few inches to half a dozen feet in diameter, with each a raised edge all around, where apparently the floating sludge has been caught and accumulated. (Occasionally the raised edge is six inches high!) This is mottled black and white and is not yet safe. It is like skating over so many rails, or the edges of saws. Now I glide over a field of white air-cells close to the surface, with coverings no thicker than egg-shells, cutting through with a sharp crackling sound. There are many of these singular spider-shaped dark places amid the white ice, where the surface water has run through some days ago.

Boys are now devoted to skating after school at night, going without their suppers.

P.M.—Skated a half-mile up Assabet and then to foot of Fair Haven Hill.

This is the first tolerable skating. Last night was so cold that the river closed up everywhere, and made good skating where there had been no ice to catch the snow of the night before. First there is the snow ice on the sides, somewhat rough and brown or yellowish spotted where the water overflowed the ice on each side yesterday, and next, over the middle, the new dark smooth ice, and, where the river is wider than usual, a thick fine gray ice, marbled, where there was probably a thin ice yesterday. Probably the top froze as the snow fell. I am surprised to find how rapidly and easily I get along, how soon I am at this brook or that bend in the river, which it takes me so long to reach on the bank or by water. I can go more than double the usual distance before dark. It takes a little while to learn to trust the new black ice. I look for cracks to see how thick it is. . . .

It is apt to be melted at the bridges about the piers, and there is a flow of water over the ice here. There is a fine, smooth gray marbled ice on the bays which apparently began to freeze when it was snowing night before last. There is a marbling of dark where was clear water amid the snow. Now and then a crack crosses it, and the water, oozing out, has frozen on each side of it two or three inches thick, and sometimes as many feet wide. These give you a slight jolt.

Fishing through ice began on Flint's and Fair Haven yesterday. The first fishers succeed best.

As I enter on Fair Haven Pond, I see already three pickerel-fishers retreating from it, drawing a sled through the Baker Farm, and see where they have been fishing, by the shining chips of ice about the holes. Others were here even yesterday, as it appears. The pond must have been frozen by the 4th at least. Some fisherman or other is ready with his reels and bait as soon as the ice will bear, whether it be Saturday or Sunday. Theirs, too, is a sort of devotion, though it be called hard names by the preacher, who perhaps could not endure the cold and wet any day. Perhaps he dines off their pickerel on Monday at the hotel. . . .

That grand old poem Winter is round again without any connivance of mine. As I sit under Lee's Cliff where the snow is melted, amid sere penny royal and frost-bitten catnep, I look over my shoulder upon an artic scene. I see with surprise the pond a dumb white surface of ice speckled with snow, just as so many winters before, where so lately were lapsing waves or smooth reflecting water. I see the holes which the pickerel-fisher has made, and I see him too, retreating over the hills, drawing his sled behind him. The water is already skimmed over again there. I hear, too, the familiar belching voice of the pond.

Heavy Haines was fishing a quarter of a mile this side of Hubbard's Bridge. He had caught a pickerel, which the man who weighed it told me, weighed four pounds and three ounces. It was twenty-six inches long. It was a very handsome fish—dark-brown above, yellow and brown on the sides, becoming at length almost a clear golden yellow low down, with a white abdomen and reddish fins. They are handsome fellows, both the pikes in the water and tigers in the jungle. The shiner and the redfinned minnow (a dace) are the favorite bait for them.

What tragedies are enacted under this dumb icy platform in the fields! What an anxious and adventurous life the small fishes must live, liable at any moment to be swallowed by the larger. No fish of moderate size can go sculling along safely in any part of the stream, but suddenly there may come rushing out of this jungle or that some greedy monster and gulp it down. Parent fishes, if they care for their offspring, how can they trust them abroad out of their sight? It takes so many young fishes a week to fill the maw of this large one. And the large ones! Heavy Haynes and Company are lying in wait for them.

Perhaps the coldest night. The pump is slightly- frozen.

7 A.M.—To Hill.

Said to be the coldest morning as yet. The river appears to be frozen everywhere. Where was water last night is a firm bridge of ice this morning. The snow which has blown on to the ice has taken the form of regular star-shaped crystals, an inch in diameter. Sometimes these are arranged in a spear three feet long quite straight. I see the mother-o'-pearl tints now, at sunrise, on the clouds high over the eastern horizon before the sun has risen above the low bank in the east. The sky in the eastern horizon has that same greenish-vitreous, gem-like appearance which it has at sundown, as if it were of perfectly clear glass—with the green tint of a large mass of glass. Here are some crows already seeking their breakfast in the orchard, and I hear a red squirrel's reproof. The woodchoppers are making haste to their work far off, walking fast to keep warm, before the sun has risen, their ears and hands well covered, the dry, cold snow squeaking under their feet. They will be warmer after they have been at work an hour.

You may walk eastward in the winter afternoon till the ice begins to look green, half to three quarters of an hour before sunset, the sun having sunk behind you to the proper angle. Then it is time to turn your steps homeward. Soon after,[2] too, the ice began to boom, or fire its evening gun, another warning that the end of the day was at hand, and a little after the snow reflected a distinct rosy light, the

---

[2] About the same time, as noticed two or three days [Thoreau].

sun having reached the grosser atmosphere of the earth.[3]
These signs successively prompt us once more to retrace
our steps. Even the fisherman, who perhaps has not observed
any sign but that the sun is ready to sink beneath the
horizon, is winding up his lines and starting for home; or
perhaps he leaves them to freeze in.

In a clear but pleasant winter day, I walk away till the
ice begins to look green and I hear it boom, or perhaps till
the snow reflects a rosy light.

I ascended Ball's Hill to see the sun set. How red its
light at this hour! I covered its orb with my hand, and let
its rays light up the fine woolen fibres of my gloves. They
were a dazzling rose-color. It takes the gross atmosphere
of earth to make this redness.

In walking across the Great Meadows today on the
snowcrust, I noticed that the fine, dry snow which was
blown over the surface of the frozen field, when I [looked]
westward over it or toward the sun, looked precisely like
steam curling up from its surface as sometimes from a
wet roof when the sun comes out after a rain.

P.M.—Skated to Fair Haven with C.

C's skates are not the best, and beside he is far from
an easy skater, so that, as he said, it was killing work for
him. Time and again the perspiration actually dropped from
his forehead on to the ice, and it froze in long icicles on
his beard. Yet he kept up his spirits and his fun, said he
[had] seen much more suffering than I, etc. etc.

It has been a glorious winter day, its elements so simple—
the sharp clear air, the white snow everywhere covering
the earth, and the polished ice. Cold as it is, the sun seems

---

[3] A few days later he recorded—"Tonight, I notice the rose-color in the
snow and the green in the ice *at the same time,* having been looking out
for them."

warmer on my back even than in summer, as if its rays met with less obstruction. And then the air is so beautifully still; there is not an insect in the air, and hardly a leaf to rustle. If there is a grub out, you are sure to detect it on the snow or ice. The shadows of the Clamshell Hills are beautifully blue as I look back half a mile at them, and in some places where the sun falls on it, the snow has a pinkish tinge.

I am surprised to find how fast the dog can run in a straight line on the ice. I am not sure that I can beat him on skates, but I can turn much shorter. It is very fine skating for the most part. All of the river that was not frozen before, and therefore not covered with snow on the 18th, is now frozen quite smoothly; but in some places for a quarter of a mile, it is uneven like frozen suds, in rounded pancakes, as when bread spews out in baking. At sundown or before, it begins to belch. It is so cold that only in one place did I see a drop of water flowing out on the ice.

I think more of skates than of the horse or locomotive as annihilators of distance, for while I am getting along with the speed of a horse, I have at the same time the satisfaction of the horse and his rider, and far more adventure and variety than if I were riding. We never cease to be surprised when we observe how swiftly the skater glides along. Just compare him with one walking or running. The walker is but a snail in comparison, and the runner gives up the contest after a few rods. The skater can afford to follow all the windings of a stream, and yet soon leaves far behind and out of sight the walker who cuts across. Distance is hardly an obstacle to him.

The snow which began last night has continued to fall very silently but steadily, and now it is not far from a foot deep, much the most we have had yet; a dry, light, powdery snow. When I come down I see it in miniature drifts against the panes, alternately streaked dark and light as it is more or less dense. A remarkable, perfectly conical peak, a foot high, with concave sides, stands in the fireplace under the sink-room chimney. The pump has a regular conical Persian (?) cap, and every post about the house a similar one. It is quite light but has not drifted. About 9 A.M. it ceases, and the sun comes out, and shines dazzlingly over the white surface. Every neighbor is shoveling out, and hear the sound the shovels scraping on door-steps. Winter now first fairly commenced, I feel.

The places which are slowest to freeze in our river are, first *on account of warmth as well as motion,* where a brook comes in, and also probably where are springs in banks and under bridges; then, on account of shallowness and rapidity, at bends. I perceive that the cold respects the same places every winter. In the dark, or after a heavy snow, I know well where to cross the river most safely. Where the river is most like a lake, broad with a deep and muddy bottom, there it freezes first and thickest.

On river to Fair Haven Pond.

A beautiful, clear, not very cold day. The shadows on the snow are indigo-blue. The pines look very dark. . . . Once a partridge rises from the alders and skims across the river at its widest part just before me; a fine sight. On the edge of A. Wheeler's cranberry meadow I see the track of an otter made since yesterday morning. How glorious the perfect stillness and peace of the winter landscape!

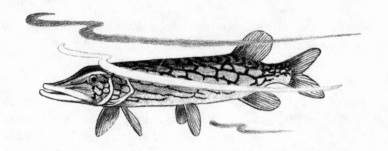

January

This is one of those pleasant winter mornings when you find the river firmly frozen in the night, but still the air is serene and the sun feels gratefully warm an hour after sunrise—though so fair, a healthy whitish vapor fills the lower stratum of the air, concealing the mountains—the smokes go up from the village, you hear the cocks with immortal vigor, and the children shout on their way to school, and the sound made by the railroad men hammering a rail is uncommonly musical. This promises a perfect winter day. In the heavens, except the altitude of the sun, you have, as it were, the conditions of summer. Perfect serenity and clarity and sonorousness in the earth. All nature is but braced by the cold. It gives tension to both body and mind.

How little locomotive now look the boats whose painted sterns I just detect where they are half filled with ice and almost completely buried in snow, so neglected by their improvident owners—some frozen in the ice, opening their

187

seams, some drawn up on the bank. This is not merely improvidence; it is ingratitude.

As I go over the causeway near the railroad bridge, I hear a fine busy twitter, and looking up, see a nuthatch hopping along and about a swamp white oak branch, inspecting every side of it, as readily hanging head downwards as standing upright, and then it utters a distinct *gnah* as if to attract a companion. Indeed, that other finer twitter seemed designed to keep some companion in tow, or else it was like a very busy man talking to himself. The companion was a single chickadee, which lisped six or eight feet off. There were, perhaps, no other birds than these two within a quarter of a mile. And when the nuthatch flitted to another tree two rods off, the chickadee unfailingly followed.

I see the dead stems of the water horehound just rising above the snow and curving outward over the bank of the Assabet, near the stone-heaps, with its brown clusters of dry seeds, etc., every inch or two. These, stripped off or rubbed between the fingers, look somewhat like ground coffee and are agreeabily aromatic. They have the fragrance of lemon peel.

The alder is one of the prettiest of trees and shrubs in the winter, it is evidently so full of life, with its conspicuous red catkins dangling from it on all sides. It seems to dread the winter less than other plants. It has a certain heyday and cheery look, and less stiff than most, with more of the flexible grace of summer. With those dangling clusters of red catkins which it switches in the face of winter, it brags for all vegetation. It is not daunted by the cold, but hangs gracefully still over the frozen stream.

I picked up on the bare ice of the river, opposite the oak in Shattuck's land, on a small space blown bare of the snow, a fuzzy caterpillar, black at the two ends and red-brown in the middle, rolled into a ball or close ring, like a woodchuck. I pressed it hard between my fingers and found it frozen. I put it into my hat, and when I took it out in the evening, it soon began to stir and at length crawled about, but a portion of it was not quite flexible. It took some time for it to thaw.

They are very different seasons in the winter when the ice of the river and meadows and ponds is bare—blue or green, a vast glittering crystal—and when it is all covered with snow or slosh; and our moods correspond. The former may be called a crystalline winter.

A fine snow has just begun to fall, so we made haste to improve the skating before it was too late. Our skates made tracks often nearly an inch broad in the slight snow which soon covered the ice. All along the shores and about the islets the water had broadly overflowed the ice of the meadows, and frequently we had to skate through it, making it fly. The snow soon showed where the water was. It was a pleasant time to skate, so still, and the air so thick with snowflakes that the outline of near hills was seen against it and not against the more distant and higher hills. Single pines stood out distinctly against it in the near horizon.

Up Assabet to bridge.

Two or more inches of snow fell last night. In the expanse this side Mantucket Rock, I see the tracks of a crow or crows in and about the button-bushes and willows. . . . You will see a crow's track beginning in the middle of the river, where one alighted. I notice such a track as this, where one

alighted and apparently struck its spread tail into the snow
at the same time with its feet. I see afterwards where a
wing's quills have marked the snow much like a partridge's.
The snow is very light, so that the tracks are rarely distinct,
and as they advance by hops some might mistake it for a
squirrel's or mink's track. I suspect that they came here
yesterday after minnows when the fishermen were gone,
and that has brought them here today in spite of the snow.
They evidently look out sharp for a morsel of fish.

Up Assabet.
The snow and ice under the hemlocks is strewn with
cones and seeds and tracked with birds and squirrels. What
a beautiful supply of winter food is here provided for them!
No sooner has fresh snow fallen and covered up the old
crop than down comes a new supply all the more distinct
on the spotless snow. Here comes a little flock of chickadees,
attracted by me as usual, and perching close by boldly;
then, descending to the snow and ice, I see them pick up
the hemlock seed which lies all around them. Occasionally
they take one to a twig and hammer at it there under their
claws, perhaps to separate it from the wing, or even the
shell. The snowy ice and the snow on shore have been
blackened with these fallen cones several times over this
winter. The snow along the sides of the river is also all
dusted over with birch and alder seed, and I see where little
birds have picked up the alder seed.

The cold spell is over, and here this morning is a fog or
mist; the wind, if there is any, I think, northerly; and there
is built out horizontally on the north side of every twig
and other surface a very remarkable sort of hoar frost, the
crystallized fog, which is still increasing. . . .
I go to the river this morning and walk up it to see the
trees and bushes along it. As the frostwork . . . is built out

northward from each surface, spreading at an angle of about forty-five degrees, *i.e.* some twenty odd each side of the north, you must stand on the north side and look south at the trees, etc., when they appear, except the large limbs and trunks, wholly of snow or frostwork, mere ghosts of trees, seen softly against the mist for background.

It is mist on mist. The outline and character of each tree is more distinctly exhibited, being exaggerated, and you notice any peculiarity in the disposition of the twigs. Some elm twigs, thus enlarged into snowy fingers, are strikingly regular and handsome. . . . In the case of most evergreens, it amounts to a very rich sugaring, being so firmly attached. The weeping willow seems to weep with more remarkable and regular curve than ever, and stands still and white with thickened twigs, as if carved in white marble or alabaster. Those trees, like alders, which have not grown much the past year—which have short and angular twigs—are the richest in effect. The end of each alder twig is recurved where the drooping catkin is concealed. On one side you see the dark brown fruit, but on the north that too is concealed.

I can see about a quarter of a mile through the mist and when later, it is somewhat thinner, the woods, the pine woods at a distance are a dark blue color.

Jan. 14. The fog-frosts and the fog continue though considerable of the frost-work has fallen.

This forenoon I walk up the Assabet to see it. The hemlocks are perhaps a richer sight than any tree—such Christmas trees, thus sugared, as were never seen. On [*sic*] side you see more or less greenness, but when you stand due north they are unexpectedly white and rich, so beautifully still, and when you look under them you see some great rock, or rocks, all hoary with the same, and a finer frost on the very fine dead hemlock twigs there and on hanging roots and twigs, quite like the cobwebs in a grist mill covered with meal—and it implies a stillness like that; or it is like the lightest down glued on. The birch, from its outline and its numerous twigs, is also one of the prettiest trees in this dress.

The fog turns to a fine rain at noon, and in the evening and night it produces a glaze, which this morning—

Jan. 15.—is quite handsome. Instead of that soft, white, faery-like mantle of down with which the trees were thickly powdered, they are now cased in a coat of mail, of icy mail, built out in many cases about as far from the twig with icy prominences. Birches, tree-tops and especially slender-twigged willows or osiers are bent over by it, as they were not by the snow-white and light frost of yesterday and the day before, so that the character of expression of many trees and shrubs is wholly altered.°

Skated to Baker Farm with a rapidity which astonished myself, before the wind, feeling the rise and fall—the water having settled in the suddenly cold night—which I had not time to see. Saw the intestines of (apparently) a rabbit— betrayed by a morsel of fur—left on the ice, probably the prey of a fox. A man feels like a new creature, a deer, perhaps, moving at this rate. He takes new possession of nature in the name of his own majesty. There was I, and there and there, as Mercury went down the Idaean Mountains. I judged that in a quarter hour I was three and a half miles from home without having made any particular exertion—*à la volaille.*

When I reached the lowest part of the Great Meadows, the neck of the Holt, I saw that the ice, thickly covered

---

° This remarkable hoar frost was akin to what the New Englander calls an ice-storm, and indeed in this instance, it was succeeded by one. Thoreau refers to the latter as a glaze.

with snow, before me was of two shades, white and darker, as far as I could see in parallel sections. This was owing to fine snow blown low over the first—hence white—portion. I noticed it when I was returning toward the sun. This snow looks just like vapor curling along over the surface—long waving lines producing the effect of a watered surface, very interesting to look at, when you face the sun, waving or curving about swellings in the ice like the grain of wood, the whole surface in motion, like a low, thin, but infinitely broad stream made up of a myriad meandering rills of vapor flowing over the surface. It *seemed* to rise a foot or two, yet when I laid my finger on the snow I did not perceive that any of the drifting snow rose above it or passed over it; it rather turned and went around it. It was the snow, probably the last light snow of the morning—when half an inch fell—blown by the strong northwest wind just risen, and apparently blown only where the surface beneath was smooth enough to let it slide. On such a surface it would evidently be blown a mile very quickly. Here the distance over which it was moving may have been half a mile. As you look down on it around you, you only see it moving straight forward in a thin sheet; but when you look at it several rods off in the sun, it has that waving or devious motion like vapor and flames, very agreeable and surprising.

On the river to Bittern Rock. . . .

In a very few places, for half a dozen feet the snow is blown off, revealing the dark transparent ice, in which I see numerous great white cleavages, which show its generous thickness, a foot at least. They cross each other at various angles and are frequently curved vertically, reflecting rainbow tints from within. Small triangles only a foot or two over are seen to be completely cracked around at the point of convulsion, yet it is as firm there as anywhere. I am proud of the strength of my floor, and love to jump and stamp there and bear my whole weight on it. As transparent as glass, yet you might found a house on it. Then there are little feathery flake-like twisted cleavages, which extend not more than an inch into it.

Up river across Cyanean Meadow.

Now we have quite another kind of ice. It has rained hard, converting into a very thin liquid the snow which had fallen on the old ice, and this, having frozen, has made a perfectly smooth but white snow ice. It is white like polished marble—I call it marble ice—and the trees and hill are reflected in it, as not in any other. It is far less varied than the other, but still is very peculiar and interesting. You notice the polished surface much more, as if it were the marble floor of some stupendous hall. Yet such is its composition it is not quite so hard and metallic, I think. The skater probably makes more of a scratch. The other was hard and crystalline.

As I look south just before sunset over this fresh and shining ice, I notice that its surface is divided, as it were, into a great many contiguous tables in different planes, somewhat like so many different facets of a polyhedron as large as the earth itself. These tables or planes are bounded by cracks, though without any appreciable opening, and the different levels are betrayed by the reflections of the light or sky being interrupted at the cracks. The ice formed last night is a day old, and these cracks, as I find, run generally from northeast to southwest across the entire meadow, some twenty-five or thirty rods, nearly at right angles with the river, and are from five to fifteen feet apart, while there are comparatively few cracks crossing them in the other direction. You notice this phenomenon looking over the ice some rods before you; otherwise might not observe the cracks when upon them. It is as if the very globe itself were a crystal with a certain number of facets.

When I look westward now to the flat snow-crusted shore, it reflects a strong violet color. Also the pink light reflected from the low, flat snowy surfaces amid the ice on the meadows, just before sunset, is a constant phenomenon these clear winter days. Whole fields and sides of hills are often the same, but it is more distinct on these flat islands of snow scattered here and there over the meadow ice. I also see this pink in the dust made by the skaters. Perhaps the green seen at the same time in ice and water is produced by the general yellow or amber light of this hour, mingled with the blue of the reflected sky? . . .

Surely the ice is a great and absorbing phenomenon.

It is now good walking on the river, for, though there has been no thaw since the snow came, a great part of it has been converted into snow ice by sinking the old ice beneath the water, and the crust of the rest is stronger than in the fields, because the snow is so shallow and has been so moist. The river is thus an advantage as a highway, not only in summer and when the ice is bare in the winter, but even when the snow lies very deep in the fields. It is invaluable to the walker, being now not only the most interesting, but, excepting the narrow and unpleasant track in the highways, the only practicable route.

The snow never lies so deep over it as elsewhere, and, if deep, it sinks the ice and is soon converted into snow ice to a great extent, beside being blown out of the river valley. Neither is it drifted here. Here, where you cannot walk at all in the summer, is better walking than elsewhere in the winter. But what a different aspect the river's brim now from what it wears in summer! I do not this moment hear an insect hum, nor see a bird, nor a flower. That museum of animal and vegetable life, a meadow, is now reduced to a uniform level of white snow, with only half a dozen kinds of shrubs and weeds rising here and there above it.

How many memorable localities in a river walk! Here is the warm wood-side; next, the good fishing bay; and next, where the old settler was drowned when crossing on the ice a hundred years ago. It is all storied.

Up river on ice 9 A.M., above Pantry. . . .
It is surprising how much room there is in nature—if a man will follow his proper path. In these broad fields, in these extensive woods, on this stretching river, I never meet a walker. Passing behind the farmhouses, I see no man out. Perhaps I do not meet so many men as I should have met three centuries ago, when the Indian hunter roamed these woods. I enjoy the retirement and solitude of an early settler. . . .

Made a roaring fire on the edge of the meadow at Ware (?) Hill in Sudbury. A piece of paper, birch bark, and dry leaves started it and then we depended on the dead maple twigs and limbs to kindle the large dead wood. Green wood will burn better than the damp and rotten wood that lies on the ground. We chose a place which afforded a prospect, but it turned out that we looked only at the fire. It made all places indifferent. The color of the coals, in a glowing heap or seen through the white ashes on the brands, like rubies. The shadows coming and going, of the flame passing over the white ashes of the brands. I burnt my eyelashes when the fire suddenly blazed up with the wind without knowing that I had come very near it.

Though our fuel was dead and rotten wood found in the snow, it made very little smoke, which may have been owing to the state of the atmosphere, clear and cold. The sound of the air or steam escaping from a brand, its sighing or dying shriek, fine and sharp as a cambric needle, is the music we hear. One half the pleasure is in making the fire. But then we should have something to cook by it. Collecting fresh fuel from time to time is very pleasant. The smoke ever and anon compelled us to move round to the opposite side. The sap which flowed from some maple boughs which I cut froze in large drops at the end. How came sap there now?

Another cold morning. Mercury down to 13° below zero. . . .

This morning, though not so cold by a degree or two as yesterday morning,[1] the cold has got more into the house, and the frost visits nooks never known to be visited before. The sheets are frozen about the sleeper's face; the teamster's beard is white with ice. Last night I felt it stinging cold as I came up the street at 9 o'clock; it bit my ears and face, but the stars shone all the brighter. The windows are all closed up with frost as if they were ground glass. . . .

P.M.—Up river on ice and snow to Fair Haven Pond.

There is a few inches of snow, perfectly level, which now for nearly a week has covered the ice. Going toward the sun you are snow-blinded. At each clump of willows on the meadow, it looks as if there were a hillock, out of which they grow. This appearance is produced by the willow twigs holding up the ice to [the] height at which it was frozen after the last thaw, about two feet above the present level. It forms a regularly rounded hillock.

We look at every track in the snow. Every little while there is the track of a fox—maybe the same one—across the river, turning aside sometimes to a muskrat's cabin, or a point of ice, where he has left some traces, and frequently the larger track of a hound, which has followed his trail.

---

[1] 18° below zero.

It is much easier and pleasanter to walk thus on the river, the snow being shallow and level, and there is no such loud squeaking or cronching of the snow as in the road, and this road is so wide that you do not feel confined in it, and you never meet travellers with whom you have no sympathy.

The river has been frozen unusually long and solidly. They have been sledding wood along the river for a quarter of a mile in front of Merriam's and past the mouth of Sam Barrett's Brook, where it is bare of snow—hard, glare ice on which there is scarcely a trace of the sled or oxen. They have sledded home a large oak which was cut down on the bank. Yet this is one of the rockiest and swiftest parts of the stream. Where I have so often stemmed the swift current, dodging the rocks with my paddle, there the heavy, slow-paced oxen, with their ponderous squeaking load, have plodded, while the teamster walked musing beside it.

Cloudy and misty. On opening the door I feel a very warm southwesterly wind, contrasting with the cooler air of the house, and find it unexpectedly wet in the street, and the manure is being washed off the ice into the gutter. It is, in fact, a January thaw. The channel of the river is quite open in many places, and in others I remark that the ice and water alternate like waves and the hollow between them. There are long reaches of open water where I look for muskrats and ducks, as I go along to Clamshell Hill. I hear the pleasant sound of running water. I see that black scum on the surface of water above the ice.

The delicious soft, spring-suggesting air—how it fills my veins with life! Life becomes again credible to me. A certain dormant life awakens in me, and I begin to love nature again. Here is my Italy, my heaven, my New England. I understand why the Indians hereabouts placed heaven in the southwest—the soft south.

January 22. [1855] Rained all night. Walking now worse than ever this year, midleg deep in gutters. Lakes in the street. River risen—a freshet—breaking up ice a foot thick, flows under dry causeway, bridges a torrent; muskrats driven out by hundreds and shot; dark angry waves where was lately ice and snow. Earth washed bare. Radical leaves appear and russet hills. Still rains a *little*.

It is very exciting to see, where so lately only ice and snow, dark wavy lakes, dashing in furious torrents through the commonly dry channels under the causeways, to hear only the rush and roar of waters and look down on mad billows where in summer is commonly only dry pebbles. Great cakes of ice lodged and sometimes titled up against the causeway bridges, over which the water pours as over a dam. After their passage under these commonly dry bridges the crowding waters are at least six or eight inches higher than those of the surrounding meadow. What a tumult at the stone bridge, where cakes of ice a rod in diameter and a foot thick are carried round and round by the eddy in circles eight or ten rods in diameter, and rarely get a chance to go down stream, while others are seen coming up edgewise from below in the midst of the torrent! The muskrats driven out of their holes by the water are exceedingly numerous, yet many of their cabins are above water on the south branch. Here there are none. We saw fifteen or twenty, at least, between Derby's Bridge and the Tarbell Spring, either swimming with surprising swiftness up or down or across the stream to avoid us, or sitting at the water's edge, or resting on the edge of the ice (one refreshed himself there after its cold swim regardless of

us, probed its fur with its nose and scratched its ear like
a dog) or on some alder bush just on the surface. They
frequently swam toward an apple tree in the midst of the
water in the vain hope of finding a resting-place and
refuge there.

*The January thaw is an annual interlude in the course
of almost every New England winter. Four years later almost to a day, Thoreau records its significant aspect on
the Concord—the musquash hunter.*

I hear these guns going today, and I must confess they
are to me a springlike and exhilarating sound, like the cock-
crowing, though each one may report the death of a musquash. . . . In the musquash-hunters I see the Almouchicois
still pushing swiftly over the dark stream in their canoes.
These aboriginal men cannot be repressed, but under some
guise or other they survive and reappear continually. Just
as simply as the crow picks up the worms which all over
the fields have been washed out by the thaw, these men
pick up the musquash that have been washed out the banks.
And to serve such ends men plow and sail, and powder and
shot are made, and the grocer exists to retail them, though
he may think himself much more the deacon of some church.

Saw A. Hosmer approaching in his pung.[2] He calculated
so that we should meet just when he reached the bare
planking of the causeway bridge, so that his horse might
as it were stop of his own accord and no other excuse
would be needed for a talk.

Walking on the ice by the side of the river this very
pleasant morning, I see many minnows (may be dace)

---

[2] A pung is a low-hung one-horse sled on heavy runners. In these days of
mechanical transport this New England localism, a corruption of the Indian
Tom-pung meaning an "instrument for drawing," bids fair to become utterly obsolete.

from one and a half to four inches long which have come
out through holes or cracks a foot wide more or less, where
the current has worn through and shows the dark stream,
and the water has flown over the adjacent ice, sinking it
down so as to form a shallow water four or five feet or
more, and often several rods long, and four or five inches
deep on the side next the crack, or deepest side. This water
has a yellowish color, and a fish or anything else in it is
at once seen. I think that they come out into this thin
water overlying the ice for the sake of the sun's warmth.
Much heat must be reflected from the icy bottom this
sunny morning—a sort of anticipation of spring to them.
This shallow surface water is also thinly frozen over, and
I can sometimes put my hand close over the minnow. When
alarmed they make haste back to the dark water of the
crack, and seek the depths again.

P.M. Up river.
The hardest day to bear that we have had, for, beside
being 5° at noon and at 4 P.M., there is a strong northwest
wind. It is worse than when the thermometer was at zero
all day. . . . I see no life abroad, no bird nor beast. What
a stern, bleak, inhospitable aspect nature now wears!—I am
off Clamshell Hill.—Where a few months since there was
a fertilizing river reflecting the sunset, and luxuriant meadows resounding with the hum of insects, is now a uniform
crusted snow, with dry powdery snow drifting over it and
confounding river and meadow. I make haste away, covering my ears, before I freeze there.

A clear, cold, beautiful day. Fine skating. An unprece-
dented expanse of ice. . . .
Before skating upstream I tried my boat sail on the
meadow in front of the house and found that I could go
well enough before the wind, resting the mast on my hip

and holding by the middle with one hand, but I could not easily tack.

The country thus almost completely bare of snow—only some ice in the roads and fields—and the frozen freshet at this remarkable height, I skated up as far as the boundary between Wayland and Sudbury just above Pelham's Pond, to a point which a woman called about one and a half miles from Saxonville, about twelve miles between 10 A.M. and one, quite leisurely. . . .

As I skated near the shore under Lee's Cliff, I saw what I took to be some crags or knotty stubs of a dead limb lying on the bank beneath a white oak, close by me. Yet while I looked directly at them I could not but admire their close resemblance to partridges. I had come along with a rapid whir and suddenly halted right against them, only two rods distant, and, as my eyes watered a little from skating against the wind, I was not convinced that they were birds till I had pulled out my glass and deliberately examined them. They sat and stood, three of them, perfectly still with their heads erect, some darker feathers like ears, methinks, increasing their resemblance to scrabs [sic], as where a small limb is broken off.

I was much surprised at the remarkable stillness they preserved, instinctively relying on the resemblance to the ground for their protection *i.e.* withered grass, dry oak leaves, dead scrags, and broken twigs. I thought at first that it was a dead oak limb with a few stub ends or scrabbs [*sic*] sticking up, and for some time after I had noticed the resemblance to birds, standing only two rods off, I could not be sure of their character on account of their perfect motionlessness, and it was not until I brought my glass to bear on them and saw their eyes distinctly glaring on me, their necks and every muscle tense with anxiety, that I was convinced. At length, on some signal which I did not perceive, they went with a whir, as if shot, off over the bushes.

This day's skating was a memorable excursion, and three days later he wrote that:

I still recur in my mind to that skate of the 31st. I was thus enabled to get a bird's-eye view of the river—to survey its length and breadth within a few hours, connect one part (one shore) with another in my mind, and realize what was going on upon it from end to end—to know the whole as I ordinarily knew a few miles of it only. I connected the chestnut-tree house near the shore in Wayland with the chimney house[3] in Billerica, Pelham's Pond with Nutting's Pond in Bellerica. There is good skating from the mouth to Saxonville, measuring in a straight line some twenty-two miles, by the river say thirty now, Concord midway.

It is all the way of one character—a meadow river, or dead stream—Musketicook—the abode of muskrats, pickerel, etc., crossed within these dozen miles each way—or thirty in all—by some twenty low wooden bridges, *sublicii pontes,* connected with the mainland by willowy causeways. Thus the long, shallow lakes divided into reaches. These long causeways all under water and ice now, only the bridges peeping out from time to time like a dry eyelid. You must look close to find them in many cases. Mere islands are they to the traveler in the waste of water and ice. Only two villages lying near the river, Concord and Wayland, and one at each end of thirty miles.

---

[3] Atkinson's? [Thoreau]

February

The swelling river was belching on a high key, from ten to eleven. Quite a musical cracking, running like chain lightning of sound athwart my course, as if the river, squeezed, thus gave its morning's milk with music. A certain congealed milkiness in the sound, like the soft action of piano keys—a little like the cry of a pigeon woodpecker —*a-week a-week,* etc. A congealed gurgling, frog-like. As I passed, the ice forced up by the water on one side suddenly settled on another with a crash, and quite a lake was formed above the ice behind me, and my successor two hours after, to his wonder and alarm, saw my tracks disappear in one side of it and come out on the other.

My seat from time to time is the springy horizontal bough of some fallen tree which is frozen into the ice, some old maple that had blown over and retained some life for a year after in the water, covered with great shaggy perforate parmelia. Lying flat, I quench my thirst where it is melted about it, blowing aside the snow-fleas. The great arundo[1] in the Sudbury meadows was all level with the ice. There was a great bay of ice stretching up the Pantry and up Larned Brook. I looked up a broad, glaring bay of ice at the last place, which seemed to reach to the base of Nobscot and almost to the horizon. Some dead maple or oak saplings, laid side by side, made my bridges by which I got on to the ice along the watery shore. It was a problem to get off, and another to get on, dry-shod.

Snowed again half an inch more in the evening, after which, at ten o'clock, the moon still obscured, I skated on the river and meadows. The water falling, the ice on the meadow occasionally settles with a crack under our weight. It is pleasant to feel these swells and valleys occasioned by the subsidence of the water, in some cases pretty abrupt. Also to hear the hollow, rumbling sound in such rolling places on the meadow where there is an empty chamber beneath, the water being entirely run out. Our skates make but little sound in this coating of snow about an inch thick, as if we had on woolen skates, and we can easily see our tracks in the night. We seem thus to go faster than before by day, not only because we do not see but feel and imagine our rapidity, but because of the impression which the mysterious muffled sound of our feet makes. In the meanwhile we hear the distant note of a hooting owl, and the distant rumbling of approaching or retreating cars sounds like a constant waterfall. Now and then we skated

---

[1] Arundo is the botanical name of a small genus of coarse, tall grasses—the true reeds.

into some chippy, crackling white ice, where a superficial puddle had run dry before freezing hard, and got a tumble.

It was a novel experience, this skating through snow, sometimes a mile without a bare spot, this blustering day. In many places a crack ran across our course where the water had oozed out, and the driving snow catching in it had formed a thick batter with a stiffish crust in which we were tripped up and measured our lengths on the ice. The few thin places were concealed, and we avoided them by our knowledge of the localities, though we sometimes saw the air-bubbles of the mid-channel through the thin ice; for the water going down, the current is increasing and eating its way through the ice. Sometimes a thicker drift, too, threw us, or a sudden unevenness in the concealed ice; but on the whole the snow was but a slight obstruction. We skated with much more facility than I had anticipated, and I would not have missed the experience for a good deal. . . .

We went up the Pantry Meadow above the old William Wheeler house, and came down this meadow again with the wind and snow dust, spreading our coat-tails, like birds, though somewhat at the risk of our necks if we had struck a foul place. I found that I could sail on a tack pretty well, trimming with my skirts. Sometimes we had to jump suddenly over some obstacle which the snow had concealed before, to save our necks. It was worth the while for one to look back against the sun and wind and see the other sixty rods off coming, floating down like a graceful demon in the midst of the broad meadow all covered and lit with the curling snow-steam, between which you saw the ice in dark, waving streaks like a mighty river Orellana braided of a myriad steaming currents—like the demon of the storm driving his flocks and herds before him. In the midst of this tide of curling snow-steam, he sweeps and surges this way and that and comes on like the spirit of the whirlwind.

At Lee's Cliff we made a fire, kindling with white pine cones, after oak leaves and twigs—else we had lost it; these saved us, for there is a resinous drop at the point of each scale—and then we forgot that we were outdoors in a blustering winter day. . . .

Looking toward the sun and wind, you saw a broad river half a mile or more in width, its whole surface lit and alive with flowing streams of snow, in form like the steam which curls along a river's surface at sunrise, and in midst of this moving world sailed down the skater, majestically, as if on the surface of water while the steam curled as high as his knees. . . .

Some little boys ten years old are as handsome skaters as I know. They sweep along with a graceful floating motion, leaning now to this side, then to that, like a marsh hawk beating the bush.

Met Sudbury Haines on the river before the Cliffs, come a-fishing. Wearing an old coat, much patched, with many colors. He represents the Indian still. The very patches in his coat and his improvident life do so. I feel that he is as essential a part, nevertheless, of our community as the lawyer in the village. He tells me that he caught three pickerel here the other day that weighed seven pounds altogether.

It is the old story. The fisherman is a natural story-teller. No man's imagination plays more pranks than his, while he is tending his reels and trotting from one to another, or watching his cork in summer. He is ever waiting for the sky to fall. He has sent out a venture. He has a ticket in the lottery of fate, and who knows what it may draw? He ever expects to catch a bigger fish yet. He is the most patient and believing of men. Who else will stand so long in wet places? When the hay maker runs to shelter, he takes down his pole and bends his steps to the river, glad

to have a leisure day. He is more like an inhabitant of
nature. The weather concerns him. He is an observor of
her phenomena.

P.M.—Skate to Pantry Brook.

Put on skates at the mouth of swamp Bridge Brook. The
ice appears to be nearly two inches thick. There are many
rough places where the crystals are very coarse, and the
old ice on the river (for I spoke of new ice since the freshet)
is uneven and covered, more or less, with the scales of a
thin ice whose water is dried up. In some places, where the
wind has been strong, the foam is frozen into great con-
centric ridges, over which with an impetus I dash. It is
hobbling and tearing work.

Just beyond the bathing place, I see the wreck of an
ice-fleet, which yesterday morning must have been very
handsome.[2] It reminds me of a vast and crowded fleet of
sloops with large slanting sails all standing to the north.
These sails are, some of them, the largest specimens of the
leaf-structure in ice that I have seen, eight or nine inches
long. Perhaps this structure is more apparent now they have
wasted so much. Their bases can be seen continuing quite
through the level ice which has formed about them, as if
the wind and waves, breaking up a thin ice, had held it
in that position while it froze in. . . .

This is a glorious winter afternoon. The clearness of a
winter day is not impaired, while the air is still and you
feel a direct heat from the sun. It is not like the relenting

---

[2] Three years previous on the identical day, Thoreau recorded that he
had seen something that was new to him:

> Every half-mile or so along the channel of the river I saw at a dis-
> tance where apparently the ice had been broken up while freezing by
> the pressure of other ice—thin cakes of ice forced up on their edges
> and reflecting the sun like so many mirrors, whole fleets of shining
> sails, giving a very lively appearance to the river—where for a dozen
> rods the flakes of ice stood on their edges, like a fleet beating up-
> stream, against the sun, a fleet of ice-boats.

of a thaw with a southerly wind. There is a bright sheen from the snow, and the ice booms a little from time to time. On those parts of the hill which are bare, I see the radical leaves of the butter-cup, mouse-ear, and the thistle.

Especially do gray rocks or cliffs with a southwest exposure attract us now, where there is warmth and dryness. The gray color is nowhere else so agreeable to us as in these rocks in the sun at this season, where I hear the trickling of water under great ice organ-pipes.

What a floor it is I glide thus swiftly over! It is a study for the slowest walker. See the shells of countless air-bubbles within and beneath it, some a yard or two in diameter. Beneath they are crowded together from the size of a dollar downward. They give the ice a white-spotted or freckled appearance. Specimens of every coin (*numismata*) from the first minting downward. I hear the pond faintly boom or mutter in a low voice, promising another spring to the fishes. . . . This thin meadow ice with yellow water under it yields a remarkable hollow sound, like a drum, as I rip over it, as if it were about to give way under me—some of that gong-like roar which I have described elsewhere—the ice being tense. . . .

To make a perfect winter day like this, you must have a clear, sparkling air, with a sheen from the snow, sufficient cold, little or no wind; and the warmth must come directly from the sun. It must not be a thawing warmth. The tension of nature must not be relaxed. The earth must be resonant if bare, and you hear the lisping tinkle of chickadees from time to time and the unrelenting steel-cold scream of a jay, unmelted, that never flows into a song, a sort of winter trumpet, screaming cold; hard tense, frozen music, like the winter sky itself; in the blue livery of winter's band. It is like a flourish of trumpets to the winter sky. There is no hint of incubation in the jay's scream. Like the creak of a cart-wheel. . . .

The sun being low, I see as I skate, reflected from the surface of the ice, flakes of rainbow somewhat like cobwebs, where the great slopes of the crystallization fall at the right angle, six inches or a foot across, but at so small an angle with the horizon that they had seemed absolutely flat and level before. Think of this kind of mosaic and tessellation for your floor! A floor made up of surfaces not absolutely level—though level to the touch of the feet and to the noonday eye—composed of crystals variously set, but just enough inclined to reflect the colors of the rainbow when the sun gets low.

Every winter skating is supplanted by walking on the surface of the frozen rivers.

Winter comes to make walking possible where there was no walking in summer. Not till winter do we take possession of the whole of our teritory. I have three great highways raying out from one centre, which is near my door. I may walk down the main river or up either of its two branches. Could any avenues be contrived more convenient? With this river I am not compelled to walk in the tracks of horses.

The weather is still clear, cold, and unrelenting. I have walked much on the river, but, ever since it froze over, it has been on a snow-clad river, or pond. They have been river walks because the snow was shallowest there. Even the meadows, on account of the firmer crust, have been more passable than the uplands. In the afternoons I have walked off freely up or down the river, without impediment or fear, looking for birds and birds' nests and the tracks of animals; and, as often as it was written over a new snow came and presented a new blank page. If it were still after it, the tracks were beautifully distinct.

We go wading through snows now up the bleak river, in the face of the cutting northwest wind and driving snow-stream, turning now this ear, then that, to the wind and our gloved hands in our bosoms or pockets. Our tracks are obliterated before we come back. How different this from sailing or paddling up the stream here in July, or poling amid the rocks!

P.M. Down river with C.

The river has not been so concealed by snow before. The snow does not merely lie level on it and on the land, so many inches deep, but great drifts, perchance beginning on the land, stretch quite across it, so that you cannot always tell where it is, for there is no greater levelness than elsewhere to betray it. In some places, where the ice is exposed, little bunches of hoar frost have formed, with perfect ribbed leaves one inch in diameter. This morning was one of the coldest in the winter. . . . We crossed the Great Meadows lengthwise, a broad level plain, roughened only by snowy waves, about two miles long and nearly half as wide. Looking back over it made me think of what I have read of Arctic explorers travelling over snow-covered ice.

The old ice is covered with a dry powdery snow about one inch deep, from which as I walk toward the sun, this perfectly clear, bright afternoon, at 3.30 o'clock, the colors of the rainbow are reflected from a myriad fine facets. It is as if the dust of diamonds and other precious stones were spread all around. The blue and red predominate. Though I distinguish these colors everywhere toward the sun, they are so much more abundantly reflected to me from two particular directions that I see two distant rays, or arms, so to call them of this rainbow-like dust, one on each side of the sun, stretching away from me and about half a dozen feet wide, the two arms including an angle of about sixty degrees. When I look from the sun, I see merely dazzling white points. I can easily see some of these dazzling grains fifteen or twenty rods distant on any side, though the facet which reflects this light cannot be more than a tenth or twelfth of an inch at most. Yet I might easily, and commonly do, overlook all this.

Returning across the river just as the sun was setting behind the Hollowell place, the ice eastward of me a few rods off, where the snow was blown off, was as green as bottle glass, seen at the right angle, though all around above and below, was one unvaried white—a vitreous glass green. Just as I have seen the river green in a winter morning. This phenomenon is to be put with the blue in the crevices of the snow.

It blowed considerably yesterday, though it is very still today, and the light, dry snow, especially on the meadow ice and the river was remarkably plowed and drifted by it, and now presents a very wild and arctic scene. Indeed, no part of our scenery is ever more arctic than the river and its meadows now, though the snow was only some three inches deep on a level. It is cold and perfectly still, and you walk over a level snowy tract. It is a sea of white waves of nearly uniform shape and size. Each drift is a low, sharp promontory directed toward the northwest, and showing which way the wind blowed with occasional small patches of bare ice amid them. It is exactly as if you walked over a solid sea where the waves rose about two feet high. These promontories have a general resemblance to one another. Many of them are perfect tongues of snow more or less curving and sharp. . . .

. . . It is such a scene as Boothia Felix may present—if that is any wilder than Concord. . . .

We walked, as usual, on the fresh track of a fox, peculiarly pointed, and sometimes the mark of two toenails in front separate from the track of the foot in very thin snow. And as we were kindling a fire on the pond by the side of the island, we saw the fox himself at the inlet of the river. He was busily examining along the sides of the pond by the button-bushes and willows, smelling in the snow. Not appearing to regard us much, he slowly explored along the shore of the pond thus, half-way round it; at Pleasant Meadow, evidently looking for mice (or moles?) in the grass of the bank, smelling in the shallow snow there amid the stubble, often retracing his steps and pausing at particular spots. He was eagerly searching for food, intent on finding some mouse to help fill his empty stomach. He had a blackish tail and blackish feet. Looked lean and stood high. The tail peculiarly large for any creature to carry round. He stepped daintily about, softly, and is more to the manor born than a dog. It was a very arctic scene this cold day, and I suppose he would hardly have ventured out in a warm one.

And today, seeing a peculiar very long track of a man in the snow, who has been along up the river this morning, I guessed that it was George Melvin, because it was accompanied by a hound's track. There was a thin snow on the ice, and I observed that he not only furrowed the snow for a foot before he completed his step, but that the (toe) of his track was always indefinite, as if his boot had been worn out and prolonged at the toe. I noticed that I and my companion made a clear and distinct track at the toe, but when I experimented and tried to make a track like this by not lifting my feet but gliding and partly scuffing along, I found myself walking like Melvin, and that perfectly convinced me that it was he.[3]

---

[3] I told him of it afterward, and he gave a corresponding account of himself [Thoreau].

Walk up river to Fair Haven Pond. Clear and windy—northwest. . . .

Above me is a cloudless blue sky; beneath, the sky-blue, *i.e.*, sky-reflecting, ice with patches of snow scattered over it like mackerel clouds. At a distance in several directions I see the tawny earth streaked or spotted with white where the bank or hills and fields appear, or else the green-black evergreen forests, or the brown, or russet, or tawny deciduous woods, and here and there, where the agitated surface of the river is exposed, the blue-black water. That dark-eyed water, especially when I see it at right angles with the direction of the sun, is it not the first sign of spring? How its darkness contrasts with the general lightness of the winter! It has more life in it than any part of the earth's surface. It is where one of the arteries of the earth is palpable, visible.

Those are peculiar portions of the river which have thus always opened first—been open latest and longest. In winter not only some creatures, but the very earth is partially dormant; vegetation ceases, and rivers, to some extent, cease to flow. Therefore, when I see the water exposed in midwinter, it is as if I saw a skunk or even a striped squirrel out. It is as if the woodchuck unrolled himself and snuffed the air to see if it were warm enough to be trusted.

It excites me to see early in the spring that black artery leaping once more through the snow-clad town, All is tumult and life there, not to mention the rails and cranberries that are drifting in it. Where this artery is shallowest, *i.e.*, comes nearest to the surface and runs swiftest, there it shows itself soonest and you may see its pulse beat. These are the wrists, temples, of the earth, where I feel its pulse with my eye. The living waters, not the dead earth. It is as if the dormant earth opened its dark and liquid eye upon us. . . .

Returning just before sunset, I see the ice beginning to be green, and a rose-color to be reflected from the low snow patches. I see the color from the snow first where there is some shade, as where the shadow of a maple falls afar over the ice and snow. From this is reflected a purple tinge when I see none elsewhere. Some shadow or twilight, then, is necessary, umbra mixed with the reflected sun. Off Holden Wood where the low rays fall on the river from between the fringe of the wood, the snow-patches are not rose-color, but a very dark purple like a grape, and thus there are all degrees from pure white to black. When crossing Hubbard's broad meadow, the snow-patches are a most beautiful crystalline purple, like the petals of some flowers, or as if tinged with cranberry juice. It is quite a faery scene, surprising and wonderful, as if you walked amid those rosy and purple clouds that you see float in the evening sky. What need to visit the crimson cliffs of Beverly.

I thus find myself returning over a green sea, winding amid purple islets, and the low sedge of the meadow on one side is really a burning yellow. . . .

I walk over a smooth green sea, or *aequor,* the sun just disappearing in the cloudless horizon amid thousands of these flat isles as purple as the petals of a flower. It would not be more enchanting to walk amid the purple clouds of the sunset sky. And, by the way, this is but a sunset sky under our feet, produced by the same law, the same slanting rays and twilight. Here the clouds are these patches of snow or frozen vapor, and the ice is the greenish sky between them. Thus all of heaven is realized on earth. You have seen those purple fortunate isles in the sunset heavens, and that green and amber sky between them. Would you believe that you could ever walk amid those isles? You can on many a winter evening. I have done so a hundred times. The ice is a solid crystalline sky under our feet.

In the shank of the winter, sometimes early, sometimes late, the spring freshet is an annual phenomenon that is faithfully recorded.

All day a steady, warm, imprisoning rain carrying off the snow, not unmusical on my roof.

Morning—rain over; water in great part run off; wind rising; river risen and meadows flooded. The rain-water and melted snow have run swiftly over the frozen ground into the river, and raised it with the ice on it and flooded the meadows, covering the ice there which remains on the bottom; so that you have on the male side,[4] the narrow canal above the ice, then a floating ice everywhere bridging the river, and then a broad meadowy flood above the ice again.

Already we begin to anticipate spring, and this is an important difference between this time and a month ago. We begin to say that the day is spring-like. Is not January the hardest month to get through? When you have weathered that, you get into the gulf-stream of winter, nearer the shores of spring.

February may be called *earine* (spring-like). There is a peculiarity in the air when the temperature is thus high and the weather fair, at this season, which makes sounds more clear and pervading, as if they trusted themselves abroad further in this genial state of the air. A different sound comes to my ear now from the iron rails which are struck, as from the cawing of crows, etc. Sound is not abrupt, piercing, or rending, but softly sweet and musical.

---

[4] Methinks there is a male and a female shore to the river, one abrupt, the other flat and meadowy—June 15, 1852.

It will take a yet more genial and milder air before the bluebird's warble can be heard.

Up Assabet.

The river having suddenly gone down since the freshet, I see cakes of ice eight or ten feet across left two feet high or more above the banks, frozen to four of five maples or oaks. Indeed, each shore is lined with them, where wooded, a continuous row attached to alders, maples, swamp white oaks, etc., which grow through them or against their edges. They are somewhat like tables of a picnic party or a muster field dinner. Rustic tables and seats. Sometimes a little inclined, having settled on one side.

The ice in the middle of this stream [Assabet] is for the most part broken up. Great cakes of ice are wedged against the railroad bridge there, and still threaten its existence. They are about twenty feet in diameter and some twenty inches thick, of greenish ice, more or less tilted up and commonly another, if not two more, of equal size, forced directly underneath the first by the current. They stretch quite across the river, and, being partly tilted up against the spiles of the bridge, exert a tremendous power upon it. They form a dam between and over which the water falls, so that it is fully ten inches higher on the upper side of the bridge than on the lower. Two maples a little above the bridge—one a large one—have been levelled and carried off by the ice. The track repairers have been at work here all day protecting the bridge. They have a man on the ice with a rope around his body—the other end in their hands—who is cracking off the corners of the cakes with a crow-bar. One great cake, as much as a dozen rods long, is slowly whirling round just above the bridge, and from time to time an end is borne against the ice which lies against the bridge. The workmen say that they had cleared the stream

here before dinner, and all this had collected since. (Now
3 P.M.)

This restless and now swollen stream has burst its icy
fetters, and as I stand looking up it westward for half a mile,
where it winds slightly under a high bank, its surface is
lit up here and there with a fine-grained silvery sparkle
which makes the river appear something celestial—more
than a terrestrial river—which might have suggested that
which surrounded the shield in Homer. If rivers come out of
their icy prison thus bright and immortal, shall I not re-
sume my spring life with joy and hope?

I find that it is an excellent walk for variety and novelty
and wildness, to keep round the edge of the meadow—the
ice not being strong enough to bear and transparent as
water—on the bare ground or snow, just between the highest water mark and the present water line—a narrow,
meandering walk, rich in unexpected views and objects.
The line of rubbish which marks the higher tides—withered
flags and reeds and twigs and cranberries—is to my eyes a
very agreeable and significant line which Nature traces
along the edge of the meadows. It is a strongly marked,
enduring natural line, which in summer reminds me that
the water has once stood over where I walk. Sometimes
the grooved trees tell the same tale. The wrecks of the
meadow, which fill a thousand coves, and tell a thousand
tales to those who can read them. Our prairial, mediter-
ranean shore. The gentle rise of water around the trees in
the meadow, where oaks and maples stand far out in the
sea, and young elms sometimes are seen standing close
around some rock which lifts its head above the water,
as if protecting it, preventing it from being washed away,
though in truth they owe their origin and preservation to
it. It first invited and detained their seed, and now pre-

serves the soil in which they grow. A pleasant reminiscence of the rise of waters, to go up one side of the river and down the other, following this way, which meanders so much more than the river itself. If you cannot go on the ice, you are then gently compelled to take this course which is on the whole more beautiful—to follow the sinuosities of the meadow. Between the highest water mark and the present water line is a space generally from a few feet to a few rods in width. When the water comes over the road, then my spirits rise—when the fences are carried away. A prairial walk.

The fields of open water amid the thin ice of the meadows are the spectacle of today. They are especially dark blue when I look southwest. Has it anything to do with the direction of the wind? It is pleasant to see high dark-blue waves half a mile off running incessantly along the edge of white ice. There the motion of the blue liquid is the most distinct. As the waves rise and fall they seem to run swiftly along the edge of the ice.

Am surprised to see this afternoon a boy collecting red maple sap from some trees behind George Hubbard's. It runs freely. The earliest sap I made to flow last year was March 14th. It must be owing to the warm weather we have had.

The river for some days has been open and its sap visibly flowing, like the maple.

I walk down the river below Flint's on the north side. The sudden apparition of this dark-blue water on the surface of the earth is exciting. I must now walk where I can see the most water, as to the most living part of nature. This is the blood of the earth, and we see its blue arteries pulsing with new life now. I see, from far over the meadows, white cakes of ice gliding swiftly down the stream—a novel sight. They are whiter than ever in this spring sun. .) . .

I had noticed for some time, far in the middle of the Great Meadows, something dazzlingly white, which I took, of course, to be a small cake of ice on its end, but now that I have climbed the pitch pine hill and can overlook the whole meadow, I see it to be the white breast of a male sheldrake accompanied perhaps by his mate (a darker one). They have settled warily in the very midst of the meadow, where the wind has blown a space of clear water for an acre or two. The aspect of the meadow is sky-blue and dark-blue, the former a thin ice, the latter the spaces of open water which the wind has made, but it is chiefly ice still.

Thus as soon as the river breaks up or begins to break up fairly, and the strong wind widening the cracks makes at length open spaces in the ice of the meadow, this hardy bird appears, and is seen sailing in the first widened crack in the ice, where it can come to water. Instead of a piece of ice I find it to be the breast of the sheldrake, which so reflects the light as to look larger than it is, steadily sailing this way and that with its companion, who is diving from time to time. They have chosen the opening farthest removed from all shores. As I look I see the ice drifting in upon them and contracting their water, till finally they have but a few square rods left, while there are forty or fifty acres near by. This is the first bird of the spring that I have seen or heard of.

A fine spring morning. The ground is almost completely bare again. There has been a frost in the night. Now, at 8.30, it is melted and wets my feet like a dew. The water on the meadow this still, bright morning is smooth as in April. I am surprised to hear the strain of a song sparrow from the riverside, and as I cross the causeway to the hill, thinking of the bluebird, I that instant hear one's note from deep in the softened air. It is already 40°, and by noon is between 50° and 60°. As the day advances I hear more bluebirds and see their azure flakes settling on the fenceposts. Their short, rich, crispy warble curls through the air. Its grain now lies parallel to the curve of the bluebird's warble, like boards of the same lot.

It *seems* to be one of those early springs of which we have heard but have never experienced. Perhaps they are fabulous.

March

Channing, talking with Minott the other day about his health, said:

"I suppose you'd like to die now."

"No," said Minott, "I've toughed it through the winter, and I want to stay and hear the bluebirds once more."

Up river on ice to Fair Haven Pond. . . .

We have this morning the clear, cold, continent sky of January. The river is frozen solidly, and I do not have to look out for openings. Now I can take that walk along the river highway and the meadow which leads me under the boughs of the maples and the swamp white oaks, etc., which in summer overhang the water. There I can now stand at my ease, and study their phenomena, amid the sweet-gale and button-bushes projecting above the snow and ice. I see the shore from the waterside. A liberal walk, so level and wide and smooth, without underbrush.

The next four passages were written in March, 1856—a winter, as Thoreau said, "so remarkable for snow and ice." This was the year when he was unable to launch his boat until early in April.

As I return by the old Merrick Bath Place, on the river,— for I still travel everywhere on the middle of the river— the setting sun falls on the osier row toward the road and attracts my attention. They certainly look brighter now and from this point than I have noticed them before this year—greenish and yellowish below and reddish above—and I fancy the sap fast flowing in their pores. Yet I think that on a close inspection I should find no change. Nevertheless, it is, on the whole, perhaps the most springlike sight I have seen.

The red maple [sap] is now about an inch deep in a quart pail—nearly all caught since morning. It now flows at the rate of about six drops in a minute. Has probably flowed faster this forenoon. It is perfectly clear, like water. Going home slipped on the ice, throwing the pail over my head to save myself, and spilt all but a pint. So it was lost on the ice of the river. When the river breaks up, it will go down the Concord into the Merrimack, and down the Merrimack into the sea, and there get salted as well as diluted, part being boiled into sugar. It suggests at any rate, what various liquors, besides those containing salt, find their way to the sea—the sap of how many kinds of trees.

It is remarkable that though I have not been able to find any open place in the river almost all winter except under the further stone bridge and at Loring's Brook—this winter so remarkable for ice and snow—Coombs should (as he says) have killed two sheldrakes at the falls by the factory, a place which I had forgotten, some four or six weeks ago. Singular that this hardy bird should have found this small opening which I had forgotten, while the ice everywhere else was from one to two feet thick, and the snow sixteen inches on the level. If there is a crack amid the rocks of some waterfall, this bright diver is sure to know it. Ask the sheldrake whether the rivers are completely sealed up.

No sooner is some opening made in the river, a square rod in area, where some brook or rill empties in, than the fishes apparently begin to seek it for light and warmth, and thus early, perchance, may become the prey of the fish hawk. They are seen to ripple the water, darting out as you approach.

Heard two hawks scream. There was something truly March-like in it, like a prolonged blast or whistling of the wind through a crevice in the sky, which like a cracked blue saucer, overlaps the woods. Such are the first rude notes which prelude the summer's quire, learned of the whistling March wind.

At Hubbard's shore where a strong but warm westerly wind is blowing, the shore is lined for half a rod in width with puverized ice, or "brash" driven against it. . . .
The noise made by this brash undulating and grating upon itself, at a little distance, is very much like the rustling of a windrow of leaves disturbed by the winds. A little farther off it is not to be distinguished from the roar of the wind in the woods.

Rivers, too, like the walker, unbutton their icy coats, and we see the dark bosoms of their channels in the midst of the ice. Again, in pools of melted snow, or where the river has risen, I look into clear, placid water, and see the russet grassy bottom in the sun. Look up or down the open channel now, so smooth, like a hibernating animal that has ventured to come out to the mouth of its burrow. One way, perhaps, it is like melted silver alloyed with copper. It goes nibbling off the edge of the thick ice on each side. Here and there I see a musquash sitting in the sun on the edge of the ice, eating a clam, and the clamshells it has left are strewn along the edge. Ever and anon he drops into the liquid mirror, and soon reappears with another clam. This clear, placid silvery water is evidently a phenomenon of spring. Winter could not show us this.

Walking by the river this afternoon, it being half open and the waves running pretty high—the black waves, yellowish where they break over the ice—I inhale a fresh, meadowy, spring odor from them which is a little exciting. It is like the fragrance of tea to an old tea-drinker.

When I get two thirds up the hill [Fair Haven], I look round and am for the hundredth time surprised by the landscape of the river valley and the horizon with its distant blue scalloped rim. It is a spring landscape, and as impossible a fortnight ago as the song of birds. It is a deeper and warmer blue than in winter, methinks. The snow is off the mountains, which seem even to have come again like the birds. The undulating river is a bright-blue channel between sharp-edged shores of ice retained by the willows. The wind blows strong but warm from west by north, so that I have to hold my paper tight when I write this, making the copses creak and roar; but the sharp tinkle of a song sparrow is heard through it all. But ah! the needles of the

pine how they shine, as I look down over the Holden wood
and westward! Every third tree is lit with the most subdued
but clear ethereal light, as if it were the most delicate frost-
work in a winter morning, reflecting no heat, but only
light. And as they rock and wave in the strong wind, even
a mile off, the light courses up and down there as over
a field of grain; *i.e.*, they are alternately light and dark,
like looms above the forest, when the shuttle is thrown between the light woof and the dark web, weaving a light
article—spring goods for Nature to wear. At sight of this
my spirit is like a lit tree.

The great phenomenon these days is the sparkling blue
water—a richer blue than the sky ever is. The flooded meadows are ripple lakes on a large scale. . . .

. . . Ever and anon the wind seems to drop down from
over the hill in strong puffs, and then spread and diffuse
itself in dark fan-shaped figures over the surface of the
water. It is glorious to see how it sports on the watery
surface. You see a hundred such nimble-footed puffs drop
and spread on all sides at once, and dash off, sweeping the
surface of the water for forty rods in [a] few seconds, as
if so many invisible spirits were playing tag there. It even
suggests some fine dust swept along just above the surface, and reminds me of snow blowing over ice and vapor
curling along a roof—meandering like that often. . . .

. . . Sometimes the wind visibly catches up the surface
and blows it along and about in spray four or five feet
high. Now and then, when the gust increases, there comes
a top of fly-away grass from over the hill, goes dancing
over the waves, and soon is lost. The requisites are high
water mostly clear of ice, ground bare and sufficiently dry,
weather warm enough, and wind strong and gusty; then
you may sit or stand on a hill and watch this play of the
wind with the water. I know of no checker-board more

interesting to watch. The wind, the gusts, comb the hair of the water-nymphs. You never tire of seeing it drop, spread, and sweep over the yielding and sensitive surface. The water is so full of life, now rising into higher billows which would make your mast crack if you had any, now subsiding into lesser, dashing against and wearing away the still anchored ice, setting many small cakes adrift.

The distant view of the open flooded Sudbury meadows, all dark blue, surrounded by a landscape of white snow, gave an impulse to the dormant sap in my veins. Dark-blue and angry waves, contrasting with the white but melting winter landscape. Ponds, of course, do not yet afford this water prospect; only the flooded meadows. There is no ice over or near the stream, and the flood has covered or broken up much of the ice on the meadows. The aspect of these waters at sunset, when the air is still, begins to be unspeakably soothing and promising. Waters are at length, and begin to reflect, and, instead of looking into the sky, I look into the placid reflecting water for the signs and promise of the morrow. These meadows are the most of ocean that I have fairly learned. Now, when the sap of the trees is probably beginning to flow, the sap of the earth, the river, overflows and bursts its icy fetters. This is the sap of which I make my sugar after the frosty nights, boiling it down and crystallizing it. I must be on the lookout now for the gulls and the ducks. That dark-blue meadowy revelation. It is as when the sap of the maple bursts forth early and runs down the trunk to the snow.

Saw two or three hawks sailing.

This morning [March 8, 1855] I got my boat out of the cellar and turned it up in the yard to let the seams open before I calk it. The blue river, now almost completely open (*i.e.*, excepting a little ice in the recesses of the shore and a good deal over the meadows), admonishes me to be swift.

March 9. . . . Painted the bottom of my boat.

P.M.—To Great Meadows.
. . . The river channel is open but there is a very *thin* ice of recent formation over the greater part of the meadows. It is a still, moist, louring day, and the water is smooth. Saw several flocks of large grayish and whitish or speckled ducks—I suppose the same that P. calls sheldrakes. They, like ducks commonly, incline to fly in a line about an equal distance apart. I hear the common sort of quacking from them. It is pleasant to see them at a distance alight on the water with a slanting flight, launch themselves, and sail along so stately.

When I reach the Assabet above the Hemlocks, I hear a loud crashing or brattling sound, and, looking through the trees, see that it is the thin ice of the night, half an hour after sunrise, now swiftly borne down the stream in large fleets and going to wreck against the thick old ice on each side. This evidently is a phenomenon of the morning.

As I stand looking over the swollen river, looking from the bridge into the flowing, eddying tide—the almost strange chocolate-colored water—the sound of distant crows and cocks is full of spring. As Anacreon says "the works of men shine," so the sounds of men and birds are musical. Something analogous to the thawing of the ice seems to have taken place in the air. At the end of winter there is a season in which we are daily expecting spring, and finally a day when it arrives. . . .
At Nut Meadow Brook crossing we rest awhile on the rail, gazing into the eddying stream. The ripple-marks on

the sandy bottom, where silver spangles shine in the river with black wrecks of caddis cases lodged under each shelving sand, the shadows of the invisible dimples reflecting prismatic colors on the bottom, the minnows already stemming the current with restless, wiggling tails, ever and anon darting aside, probably to secure some invisible mote in the water, whose shadows we do not at first detect on the sandy bottom—when detected so much more obvious as well as larger and more interesting than the substance—in which each fin is distinctly seen, though scarcely to be detected in the substance; these are all very beautiful and exhilarating sights, a sort of diet drink to heal our winter discontent. . . .

What was that sound that came on the softened air? It was the warble of the first bluebird from that scraggy apple orchard yonder. When this is heard, then has spring arrived.[1]

6 A.M.—By riverside I hear the song of many song sparrows, the most of a song of any yet. And on the swamp white oak by the stone bridge, I see and hear a red-wing. It sings almost steadily on its perch there, sitting all alone, as if to attract companions (and I see two more, also solitary, on different tree tops within a quarter of a mile), calling the river to life and tempting the ice to melt and trickle like its own sprayey notes. Another flies over on high, with a *tchuck* and at length a clear whistle. The birds anticipate the spring; they come to melt the ice with their songs.

When you walk over bare lichen-clad hills, just beginning to be dry, and look afar over the blue water on the

---

[1] But the next day's entry, March 11, 1853, commences:
  Last night it snowed, a sleety snow again, and now the ground is whitened with it, and where are gone the bluebirds whose warble was wafted to me so lately like a blue wavelet through the air.

meadows, you are beginning to break up your winter quarters and plan adventures for the new year. The scenery is like, yet unlike, November. You have the same barren russet, but now, instead of a dry, hard, cold wind, a peculiar soft, moist air or else a raw wind. Now is the reign of water. I see many crows on the meadow by the water's edge these days. It is astonishing how soon the ice has gone out of the river, but it still lies on the bottom of the meadow. Is it peculiar to the song sparrow to dodge behind and hide in walls and the like? Toward night the water becomes smooth and beautiful. Men are eager to launch their boats and paddle over the meadows.

Two ducks in river, good size, white beneath with black heads as they go over.[2] They first rise some distance downstream, and fly by on high, reconnoitering me, and I first see them on wing; then settle a quarter of a mile above by a long slanting flight, at last opposite the swimming-elm below Flint's. I come up on the bank with the sun in my face; start them again. Again they fly downstream by me on high, turn and come round back by me again with outstretched heads, and go up to the Battle-ground before they alight. Thus the river is no sooner fairly open than they are back again—before I have got my boat launched, and long before the river has worn through Fair Haven Pond.

March 14, P.M.—Repairing my boat.

The river is still rising. It is open (?) and generally over the meadows. The meadow ice is rapidly breaking up. Great cakes half a dozen rods long are drifted down against the bridges. There is a strong current on the meadow, not

---

[2] Sheldrakes? [Thoreau]

only north along the causeway, but south along the north
end of the causeway, the water thus rushing both ways
toward the only outlet at the bridge. This is proved by
great cakes of ice floating swiftly parallel with the causeway, but in opposite directions to meet at the bridge. They
are there soon broken up by the current after they strike
the abutments. I see a large cake eight feet wide and ten
inches thick, just broken off, carried under the bridge in
a vertical position and wholly under water, such is the
pressure there. This shows to what an extent the causeways
and bridges act as dams to the flood.

This afternoon I throw off my outside coat. A mild spring
day. I must hie to the Great Meadows. The air is full of
bluebirds. The ground almost entirely bare. The villagers
are out in the sun, and every man is happy whose work
takes him outdoors. I go by Sleepy Hollow toward the
Great Fields. I lean over a rail to hear what is in the air,
liquid with bluebirds' warble.

March 19. A fine clear and warm day for the season.
Launched my boat.

P.M.—Paddled to Fair Haven Pond. . . .

Already Farrar is out with his boat looking for spring
cranberries, and here comes, slowly paddling, the dark-
faced trapper Melvin with his dog and gun. I see a poor
drowned gray rabbit floating, back up as in life, but three
quarters submerged. I see a hawk circling over a small
maple grove through this calm air, ready to pounce on the
first migrating sparrow that may have arrived. . . .

The wind has got round more to the east now, at 5 P.M.,
and is raw and disagreeable, and produces a bluish haze
or mist at once in the air. It is early for such a phenomenon. *Smelled* muskrats in two places, and saw two. Saw,
by their white droppings on the bottom, where ducks had

fed. I hear at last the *tchuck tchuck* of a blackbird and, looking up, see him flying high over the river southwesterly —the wrong way—in great haste to reach somewhere; and when I reached my landing I hear my first bluebird [1855], somewhere about Cheney's trees by the river. I hear him out of the blue deeps, but do not yet see his blue body. He comes with a warble. Now first generally heard in the village. . . .

March 20. A flurry of snow at 7 A.M. I go to turn my boat up. Four or five song sparrows are flitting along amid the willows by the waterside. Probably they came yesterday with the bluebirds. From distant trees and bushes I hear a faint tinkling *te te te te te* and at last a full strain whose rhythm is *whit whit whit, ter tche, tchear tche,* deliberately sung, or measuredly, while the falling snow is beginning to whiten the ground—not discouraged by such a reception. The bluebird, too, is in the air, and I detect its blue back for a moment upon a picket.

I meet Goodwin paddling up the still, dark river on his first voyage to Fair Haven for the season. . . .
While Emerson sits writing [in] his study this still over-cast, moist day, Goodwin is paddling up the still, dark river. . . . I hear the report of his gun from time to time for an hour, heralding the death of a muskrat and reverberating far down the river.

Another fine morning.
Willows and alders along watercourses all alive these mornings and ringing with the trills and jingles and warbles of birds, even as the waters have lately broken loose and tinkle below—song sparrows, blackbirds, not to mention robins, etc., etc. The song sparrows are very abundant, peopling each bush, willow or alder for a quarter of a mile,

and pursuing each other as if now selecting their mates. It is their song which especially fills the air, made an incessant and undistinguishable trill and jingle by their numbers. I see ducks afar, sailing on the meadow, leaving a long furrow in the water behind them. Watch them at leisure without scaring them, with my glass; observe their free and undisturbed motions.

March 20 . . . [1860]—This is a slight, dripping, truly April-like rain. You hardly know whether to open your umbrella or not. More mist than rain; no wind, and the water perfectly smooth and dark, but ever and anon the cloud or mist thickens and darkens on one side, and there is a sudden rush of warm rain, which will start the grass. I stand on Hunt's Bridge and, looking up-stream, see now first, in this April rain, the water being only rippled by the current, those alternate dark and light patches on the surface, all alike dimpled with the falling drops.

Concordance

The ensuing tabulation will enable the reader to locate in the fourteen volumes of the Journal the passages that have been selected for presentation in The River. As in the other volumes in this series in this connection the courtesy of the Houghton Mifflin Company is acknowledged.

MAY